ECONOMIC JUSTICE FOR ALL

Pastoral Letter on Catholic Social Teaching and the U.S. Economy

National Conference of Catholic Bishops • Washington, D.C.

P9-BZS-148

Following the November 1980 general meeting of the National Conference of Catholic Bishops, an ad hoc committee was appointed to draft a pastoral letter on the U.S. economy. The first draft of this letter was submitted to the bishops in November 1984, with subsequent drafts presented and discussed in November 1985 and June 1986. Approval of the text by the body of bishops was given during the plenary assembly in Washington, D.C. in November 1986. Accordingly, publication of this pastoral letter, *Economic Justice for All: Catholic Social Teaching and the U.S. Economy*, is authorized by the undersigned.

Monsignor Daniel F. Hoye
General Secretary
November 18, 1986   NCCB/USCC

Cover Design: Design Network, Inc.; Washington, D.C.

Excerpts from *The Documents of Vatican II*, Walter M. Abbott, SJ, General Editor, Copyright © 1966, American Press, Inc., 106 West 56th Street, New York, N.Y. are reprinted with permission. All rights reserved.

Excerpts from *Vatican Council II: The Conciliar and Post Conciliar Documents*, Austin P. Flannery, ed. (Collegeville, Minn.: Liturgical Press, 1975) are reprinted with permission. All rights reserved.

Unless otherwise noted, Old Testament scriptural excerpts in this book are from *The New American Bible*, copyright © 1970, Confraternity of Christian Doctrine, Washington, D.C.; New Testament scriptural excerpts are from *The New American Bible*, copyright © 1986, Confraternity of Christian Doctrine, Washington, D.C. Both are used with the permission of the copyright owner.

ISBN 1-55586-101-6

Copyright © 1986
United States Catholic Conference, Inc.
Washington, D.C.
All rights reserved.

CONTENTS

A Pastoral Message

ECONOMIC JUSTICE FOR ALL

Brothers and Sisters in Christ:

1. We are believers called to follow Our Lord Jesus Christ and proclaim his Gospel in the midst of a complex and powerful economy. This reality poses both opportunities and responsibilities for Catholics in the United States. Our faith calls us to measure this economy, not only by what it produces, but also by how it touches human life and whether it protects or undermines the dignity of the human person. Economic decisions have human consequences and moral content; they help or hurt people, strengthen or weaken family life, advance or diminish the quality of justice in our land.

2. This is why we have written *Economic Justice for All: A Pastoral Letter on Catholic Social Teaching and the U.S. Economy*. This letter is a personal invitation to Catholics to use the resources of our faith, the strength of our economy, and the opportunities of our democracy to shape a society that better protects the dignity and basic rights of our sisters and brothers, both in this land and around the world.

3. The pastoral letter has been a work of careful inquiry, wide consultation, and prayerful discernment. The letter has been greatly enriched by this

process of listening and refinement. We offer this introductory pastoral message to Catholics in the United States seeking to live their faith in the marketplace—in homes, offices, factories, and schools; on farms and ranches; in boardrooms and union halls; in service agencies and legislative chambers. We seek to explain why we wrote the pastoral letter, to introduce its major themes, and to share our hopes for the dialogue and action it might generate.

Why We Write

4. We write to share our teaching, to raise questions, to challenge one another to live our faith in the world. We write as heirs of the biblical prophets who summon us "to do the right, and to love goodness, and to walk humbly with your God" (Mi 6:8). We write as followers of Jesus who told us in the Sermon on the Mount: "Blessed are the poor in spirit. . . . Blessed are the meek. . . . Blessed are they who hunger and thirst for righteousness. . . . You are the salt of the earth. . . . You are the light of the world" (Mt 5:1-6,13-14). These words challenge us not only as believers but also as consumers, citizens, workers, and owners. In the parable of the Last Judgment, Jesus said, "For I was hungry and you gave me food, I was thirsty and you gave me drink. . . . As often as you did it for one of my least brothers, you did it for me" (Mt 25:35-40). The challenge for us is to discover in our own place and time what it means to be "poor in spirit" and "the salt of the earth" and what it means to serve "the least among us" and to "hunger and thirst for righteousness."

5. Followers of Christ must avoid a tragic separation between faith and everyday life. They can neither shirk their earthly duties nor, as the Second Vatican

Council declared, "immerse [them]selves in earthly activities as if these latter were utterly foreign to religion, and religion were nothing more than the fulfillment of acts of worship and the observance of a few moral obligations" (*Pastoral Constitution on the Church in the Modern World*, no. 43).

6. Economic life raises important social and moral questions for each of us and for society as a whole. Like family life, economic life is one of the chief areas where we live out our faith, love our neighbor, confront temptation, fulfill God's creative design, and achieve our holiness. Our economic activity in factory, field, office, or shop feeds our families—or feeds our anxieties. It exercises our talents—or wastes them. It raises our hopes—or crushes them. It brings us into cooperation with others—or sets us at odds. The Second Vatican Council instructs us "to preach the message of Christ in such a way that the light of the Gospel will shine on all activities of the faithful" (*Pastoral Constitution*, no. 43). In this case, we are trying to look at economic life through the eyes of faith, applying traditional church teaching to the U.S. economy.

7. In our letter, we write as pastors, not public officials. We speak as moral teachers, not economic technicians. We seek not to make some political or ideological point but to lift up the human and ethical dimensions of economic life, aspects too often neglected in public discussion. We bring to this task a dual heritage of Catholic social teaching and traditional American values.

8. As *Catholics*, we are heirs of a long tradition of thought and action on the moral dimensions of economic activity. The life and words of Jesus and the teaching of his Church call us to serve those in need and to work actively for social and economic justice. As a community of believers, we know that our faith is tested by the quality of justice among us, that we can best measure our life together by how the poor

and the vulnerable are treated. This is not a new concern for us. It is as old as the Hebrew prophets, as compelling as the Sermon on the Mount, and as current as the powerful voice of Pope John Paul II defending the dignity of the human person.

9. As *Americans*, we are grateful for the gift of freedom and committed to the dream of "liberty and justice for all." This nation, blessed with extraordinary resources, has provided an unprecedented standard of living for millions of people. We are proud of the strength, productivity, and creativity of our economy, but we also remember those who have been left behind in our progress. We believe that we honor our history best by working for the day when all our sisters and brothers share adequately in the American dream.

10. As bishops, in proclaiming the Gospel for these times we also manage institutions, balance budgets, meet payrolls. In this we see the human face of our economy. We feel the hurts and hopes of our people. We feel the pain of our sisters and brothers who are poor, unemployed, homeless, living on the edge. The poor and vulnerable are on our doorsteps, in our parishes, in our service agencies, and in our shelters. We see too much hunger and injustice, too much suffering and despair, both in our own country and around the world.

11. As pastors, we also see the decency, generosity, and vulnerability of our people. We see the struggles of ordinary families to make ends meet and to provide a better future for their children. We know the desire of managers, professionals, and business people to shape what they do by what they believe. It is the faith, good will, and generosity of our people that gives us hope as we write this letter.

Principal Themes of the Pastoral Letter

12. The pastoral letter is not a blueprint for the American economy. It does not embrace any particular theory of how the economy works, nor does it attempt to resolve the disputes between different schools of economic thought. Instead, our letter turns to Scripture and to the social teachings of the Church. There, we discover what our economic life must serve, what standards it must meet. Let us examine some of these basic moral principles.

13. *Every economic decision and institution must be judged in light of whether it protects or undermines the dignity of the human person.* The pastoral letter begins with the human person. We believe the person is sacred—the clearest reflection of God among us. Human dignity comes from God, not from nationality, race, sex, economic status, or any human accomplishment. We judge any economic system by what it does *for* and *to* people and by how it permits all to *participate* in it. The economy should serve people, not the other way around.

14. *Human dignity can be realized and protected only in community.* In our teaching, the human person is not only sacred but also social. How we organize our society—in economics and politics, in law and policy—directly affects human dignity and the capacity of individuals to grow in community. The obligation to "love our neighbor" has an individual dimension, but it also requires a broader social commitment to the common good. We have many partial ways to measure and debate the health of our economy: Gross National Product, per capita income, stock market prices, and so forth. The Christian vision of economic life looks beyond them all and asks, Does economic

life enhance or threaten our life together as a community?

15. *All people have a right to participate in the economic life of society.* Basic justice demands that people be assured a minimum level of participation in the economy. It is wrong for a person or group to be excluded unfairly or to be unable to participate or contribute to the economy. For example, people who are both able and willing, but cannot get a job are deprived of the participation that is so vital to human development. For, it is through employment that most individuals and families meet their material needs, exercise their talents, and have an opportunity to contribute to the larger community. Such participation has a special significance in our tradition because we believe that it is a means by which we join in carrying forward God's creative activity.

16. *All members of society have a special obligation to the poor and vulnerable.* From the Scriptures and church teaching, we learn that the justice of a society is tested by the treatment of the poor. The justice that was the sign of God's covenant with Israel was measured by how the poor and unprotected—the widow, the orphan, and the stranger—were treated. The kingdom that Jesus proclaimed in his word and ministry excludes no one. Throughout Israel's history and in early Christianity, the poor are agents of God's transforming power. "The Spirit of the Lord is upon me, therefore he has anointed me. He has sent me to bring glad tidings to the poor"(Lk 4:18). This was Jesus' first public utterance. Jesus takes the side of those most in need. In the Last Judgment, so dramatically described in St. Matthew's Gospel, we are told that we will be judged according to how we respond to the hungry, the thirsty, the naked, the stranger. As followers of Christ, we are challenged to make a fundamental "option for the poor"—to speak for the voiceless, to defend the defenseless, to assess life

styles, policies, and social institutions in terms of their impact on the poor. This "option for the poor" does not mean pitting one group against another, but rather, strengthening the whole community by assisting those who are most vulnerable. As Christians, we are called to respond to the needs of *all* our brothers and sisters, but those with the greatest needs require the greatest response.

17. *Human rights are the minimum conditions for life in community.* In Catholic teaching, human rights include not only civil and political rights but also economic rights. As Pope John XXIII declared, "all people have a right to life, food, clothing, shelter, rest, medical care, education, and employment." This means that when people are without a chance to earn a living, and must go hungry and homeless, they are being denied basic rights. Society must ensure that these rights are protected. In this way, we will ensure that the minimum conditions of economic justice are met for all our sisters and brothers.

18. *Society as a whole, acting through public and private institutions, has the moral responsibility to enhance human dignity and protect human rights.* In addition to the clear responsibility of private institutions, government has an essential responsibility in this area. This does not mean that government has the primary or exclusive role, but it does have a positive moral responsibility in safeguarding human rights and ensuring that the minimum conditions of human dignity are met for all. In a democracy, government is a means by which we can act together to protect what is important to us and to promote our common values.

19. These six moral principles are not the only ones presented in the pastoral letter, but they give an overview of the moral vision that we are trying to share. This vision of economic life cannot exist in a vacuum; it must be translated into concrete measures. Our pastoral letter spells out some specific applications of

Catholic moral principles. We call for a new national commitment to full employment. We say it is a social and moral scandal that one of every seven Americans is poor, and we call for concerted efforts to eradicate poverty. The fulfillment of the basic needs of the poor is of the highest priority. We urge that all economic policies be evaluated in light of their impact on the life and stability of the family. We support measures to halt the loss of family farms and to resist the growing concentration in the ownership of agricultural resources. We specify ways in which the United States can do far more to relieve the plight of poor nations and assist in their development. We also reaffirm church teaching on the rights of workers, collective bargaining, private property, subsidiarity, and equal opportunity.

20. We believe that the recommendations in our letter are reasonable and balanced. In analyzing the economy, we reject ideological extremes and start from the fact that ours is a "mixed" economy, the product of a long history of reform and adjustment. We know that some of our specific recommendations are controversial. As bishops, we do not claim to make these prudential judgments with the same kind of authority that marks our declarations of principle. But, we feel obliged to teach by example how Christians can undertake concrete analysis and make specific judgments on economic issues. The Church's teachings cannot be left at the level of appealing generalities.

21. In the pastoral letter, we suggest that the time has come for a "New American Experiment"—to implement economic rights, to broaden the sharing of economic power, and to make economic decisions more accountable to the common good. This experiment can create new structures of economic partnership and participation within firms at the regional level, for the whole nation, and across borders.

22. Of course, there are many aspects of the economy the letter does not touch, and there are basic questions it leaves to further exploration. There are also many specific points on which men and women of good will may disagree. We look for a fruitful exchange among differing viewpoints. We pray only that all will take to heart the urgency of our concerns; that together we will test our views by the Gospel and the Church's teaching; and that we will listen to other voices in a spirit of mutual respect and open dialogue.

A Call to Conversion and Action

23. We should not be surprised if we find Catholic social teaching to be demanding. The Gospel is demanding. We are always in need of conversion, of a change of heart. We are richly blessed, and as St. Paul assures us, we are destined for glory. Yet, it is also true that we are sinners; that we are not always wise or loving or just; that, for all our amazing possibilities, we are incompletely born, wary of life, and hemmed in by fears and empty routines. We are unable to entrust ourselves fully to the living God, and so we seek substitute forms of security in material things, in power, in indifference, in popularity, in pleasure. The Scriptures warn us that these things can become forms of idolatry. We know that, at times, in order to remain truly a community of Jesus' disciples, we will have to say "no" to certain aspects in our culture, to certain trends and ways of acting that are opposed to a life of faith, love, and justice. Changes in our hearts lead naturally to a desire to change how we act. With what care, human kindness, and justice do I conduct myself at work? How will my economic decisions to buy, sell, invest, divest, hire, or fire serve human dignity and the common good? In what career can I

best exercise my talents so as to fill the world with the Spirit of Christ? How do my economic choices contribute to the strength of my family and community, to the values of my children, to a sensitivity to those in need? In this consumer society, how can I develop a healthy detachment from things and avoid the temptation to assess who I am by what I have? How do I strike a balance between labor and leisure that enlarges my capacity for friendships, for family life, for community? What government policies should I support to attain the well-being of all, especially the poor and vulnerable?

24. The answers to such questions are not always clear—or easy to live out. But, conversion is a lifelong process. And, it is not undertaken alone. It occurs with the support of the whole believing community, through baptism, common prayer, and our daily efforts, large and small, on behalf of justice. As a Church, we must be people after God's own heart, bonded by the Spirit, sustaining one another in love, setting our hearts on God's kingdom, committing ourselves to solidarity with those who suffer, working for peace and justice, acting as a sign of Christ's love and justice in the world. The Church cannot redeem the world from the deadening effects of sin and injustice unless it is working to remove sin and injustice in its own life and institutions. All of us must help the Church to practice in its own life what it preaches to others about economic justice and cooperation.

25. The challenge of this pastoral letter is not merely to think differently, but also to act differently. A renewal of economic life depends on the conscious choices and commitments of individual believers who practice their faith in the world. The road to holiness for most of us lies in our secular vocations. We need a spirituality that calls forth and supports lay initiative and witness not just in our churches but also in business, in the labor movement, in the professions, in

education, and in public life. Our faith is not just a weekend obligation, a mystery to be celebrated around the altar on Sunday. It is a pervasive reality to be practiced every day in homes, offices, factories, schools, and businesses across our land. We cannot separate what we believe from how we act in the marketplace and the broader community, for this is where we make our primary contribution to the pursuit of economic justice.

26. We ask each of you to read the pastoral letter, to study it, to pray about it, and match it with your own experience. We ask you to join with us in service to those in need. Let us reach out personally to the hungry and the homeless, to the poor and the powerless, and to the troubled and the vulnerable. In serving them, we serve Christ. Our service efforts cannot substitute for just and compassionate public policies, but they can help us practice what we preach about human life and human dignity.

27. The pursuit of economic justice takes believers into the public arena, testing the policies of government by the principles of our teaching. We ask you to become more informed and active citizens, using your voices and votes to speak for the voiceless, to defend the poor and the vulnerable and to advance the common good. We are called to shape a constituency of conscience, measuring every policy by how it touches the least, the lost, and the left-out among us. This letter calls us to conversion and common action, to new forms of stewardship, service, and citizenship.

28. The completion of a letter such as this is but the beginning of a long process of education, discussion, and action. By faith and baptism, we are fashioned into new creatures, filled with the Holy Spirit and with a love that compels us to seek out a new profound relationship with God, with the human family, and with all created things. Jesus has entered our

history as God's anointed son who announces the coming of God's kingdom, a kingdom of justice and peace and freedom. And, what Jesus proclaims, he embodies in his actions. His ministry reveals that the reign of God is something more powerful than evil, injustice, and the hardness of hearts. Through his crucifixion and resurrection, he reveals that God's love is ultimately victorious over all suffering, all horror, all meaninglessness, and even over the mystery of death. Thus, we proclaim words of hope and assurance to all who suffer and are in need.

29. We believe that the Christian view of life, including economic life, can transform the lives of individuals, families, schools, and our whole culture. We believe that with your prayers, reflection, service, and action, our economy can be shaped so that human dignity prospers and the human person is served. This is the unfinished work of our nation. This is the challenge of our faith.

Chapter I

THE CHURCH AND THE FUTURE OF THE U.S. ECONOMY

1. Every perspective on economic life that is human, moral, and Christian must be shaped by three questions: What does the economy do *for* people? What does it do *to* people? And how do people *participate* in it? The economy is a human reality: men and women working together to develop and care for the whole of God's creation. All this work must serve the material and spiritual well-being of people. It influences what people hope for themselves and their loved ones. It affects the way they act together in society. It influences their very faith in God.[1]

2. The Second Vatican Council declared that "the joys and hopes, the griefs and anxieties of the people of this age, especially those who are poor or in any way afflicted, these too are the joys and hopes, the griefs and anxieties of the followers of Christ."[2] There are many signs of hope in U.S. economic life today:

---

[1] Vatican Council II, *The Pastoral Constitution on the Church in the Modern World*, 33. [Note: This pastoral letter frequently refers to documents of the Second Vatican Council, papal encyclicals, and other official teachings of the Roman Catholic Church. Most of these texts have been published by the United States Catholic Conference Office of Publishing and Promotion Services; many are available in collections, though no single collection is comprehensive. See Selected Bibliography.]

[2] *Pastoral Constitution*, 1.

1

- Many fathers and mothers skillfully balance the arduous responsibilities of work and family life. There are parents who pursue a purposeful and modest way of life and by their example encourage their children to follow a similar path. A large number of women and men, drawing on their religious tradition, recognize the challenging vocation of family life and child rearing in a culture that emphasizes material display and self-gratification.
- Conscientious business people seek new and more equitable ways to organize resources and the workplace. They face hard choices over expanding or retrenching, shifting investments, hiring or firing.
- Young people choosing their life's work ask whether success and security are compatible with service to others.
- Workers whose labor may be toilsome or repetitive try daily to ennoble their work with a spirit of solidarity and friendship.
- New immigrants brave dislocations while hoping for the opportunities realized by the millions who came before them.

3. These signs of hope are not the whole story. There have been failures—some of them massive and ugly:

- Poor and homeless people sleep in community shelters and in our church basements; the hungry line up in soup lines.
- Unemployment gnaws at the self-respect of both middle-aged persons who have lost jobs and the young who cannot find them.
- Hardworking men and women wonder if the system of enterprise that helped them yesterday might destroy their jobs and their communities tomorrow.

- Families confront major new challenges: dwindling social supports for family stability; economic pressures that force both parents of young children to work outside the home; a driven pace of life among the successful that can sap love and commitment; lack of hope among those who have less or nothing at all. Very different kinds of families bear different burdens of our economic system.
- Farmers face the loss of their land and way of life; young people find it difficult to choose farming as a vocation; farming communities are threatened; migrant farmworkers break their backs in serf-like conditions for disgracefully low wages.

4. *And beyond our own shores, the reality of 800 million people living in absolute poverty and 450 million malnourished or facing starvation casts an ominous shadow over all these hopes and problems at home.*

5. Anyone who sees all this will understand our concern as pastors and bishops. People shape the economy and in turn are shaped by it. Economic arrangements can be sources of fulfillment, of hope, of community—or of frustration, isolation, and even despair. They teach virtues—or vices—and day by day help mold our characters. They affect the quality of people's lives; at the extreme even determining whether people live or die. Serious economic choices go beyond purely technical issues to fundamental questions of value and human purpose.[3] We believe that in facing these questions the Christian religious and moral tradition can make an important contribution.

---

[3] See ibid., 10, 42, 43; Congregation for the Doctrine of the Faith, *Instruction on Christian Freedom and Liberation,* (Washington, D.C.: USCC Office of Publishing and Promotion Services, 1986), 34-36.

A. The U.S. Economy Today: Memory and Hope

6. The United States is among the most economically powerful nations on earth. In its short history the U.S. economy has grown to provide an unprecedented standard of living for most of its people. The nation has created productive work for millions of immigrants and enabled them to broaden their freedoms, improve their families' quality of life, and contribute to the building of a great nation. Those who came to this country from other lands often understood their new lives in the light of biblical faith. They thought of themselves as entering a promised land of political freedom and economic opportunity. The United States *is* a land of vast natural resources and fertile soil. It *has* encouraged citizens to undertake bold ventures. Through hard work, self-sacrifice, and cooperation, families have flourished; towns, cities, and a powerful nation have been created.

7. But we should recall this history with sober humility. The American experiment in social, political, and economic life has involved serious conflict and suffering. Our nation was born in the face of injustice to native Americans, and its independence was paid for with the blood of revolution. Slavery stained the commercial life of the land through its first two hundred and fifty years and was ended only by a violent civil war. The establishment of women's suffrage, the protection of industrial workers, the elimination of child labor, the response to the Great Depression of the 1930s, and the civil rights movement of the 1960s all involved a sustained struggle to transform the political and economic institutions of the nation.

8. The U.S. value system emphasizes economic freedom. It also recognizes that the market is limited

4

by fundamental human rights. Some things are never to be bought or sold.[4] This conviction has prompted positive steps to modify the operation of the market when it harms vulnerable members of society. Labor unions help workers resist exploitation. Through their government, the people of the United States have provided support for education, access to food, unemployment compensation, security in old age, and protection of the environment. The market system contributes to the success of the U. S. economy, but so do many efforts to forge economic institutions and public policies that enable *all* to share in the riches of the nation. The country's economy has been built through a creative struggle; entrepreneurs, business people, workers, unions, consumers, and government have all played essential roles.

9. The task of the United States today is as demanding as that faced by our forebears. Abraham Lincoln's words at Gettysburg are a reminder that complacency today would be a betrayal of our nation's history: "It is for us, the living, rather to be dedicated here to the unfinished work . . . they have thus far nobly advanced."[5] There is unfinished business in the American experiment in freedom and justice for all.

---

[4] See Pope John Paul II, *On Human Work* (1981), 14; and Pope Paul VI, *Octogesima Adveniens* (1971), 35. See also Arthur Okun, *Equality and Efficiency: The Big Tradeoff* (Washington, D.C.: The Brookings Institution, 1975), ch. 1; Michael Walzer, *Spheres of Justice: A Defense of Pluralism and Equality* (New York: Basic Books, 1983), ch. 4; Jon P. Gunnemann, "Capitalism and Commutative Justice," paper presented at the 1985 meeting of the Society of Christian Ethics.

[5] Abraham Lincoln, Address at Dedication of National Cemetery at Gettysburg, November 19, 1863.

B. Urgent Problems of Today

10. The preeminent role of the United States in an increasingly interdependent global economy is a central sign of our times.[6] The United States is still the world's economic giant. Decisions made here have immediate effects in other countries; decisions made abroad have immediate consequences for steelworkers in Pittsburgh, oil company employees in Houston, and farmers in Iowa. U.S. economic growth is vitally dependent on resources from other countries and on their purchases of our goods and services. Many jobs in U.S. industry and agriculture depend on our ability to export manufactured goods and food.

11. In some industries the mobility of capital and technology makes wages the main variable in the cost of production. Overseas competitors with the same technology but with wage rates as low as one-tenth of ours put enormous pressure on U.S. firms to cut wages, relocate abroad, or close. U.S. workers and their communities should not be expected to bear these burdens alone.

12. All people on this globe share a common ecological environment that is under increasing pressure. Depletion of soil, water, and other natural resources endangers the future. Pollution of air and water threatens the delicate balance of the biosphere on which future generations will depend.[7] The resources of the earth have been created by God for the benefit of all, and we who are alive today hold them in trust. This is a challenge to develop a new ecological ethic that will help shape a future that is both just and sustainable.

---

[6] Pope John XXIII, *Peace on Earth* (1963), 130-131.

[7] Synod of Bishops, *Justice in the World* (1971), 8; Pope John Paul II, *Redeemer of Man* (1979), 15.

6

13. In short, nations separated by geography, culture, and ideology are linked in a complex commercial, financial, technological, and environmental network. These links have two direct consequences. First, they create hope for a new form of community among all peoples, one built on dignity, solidarity, and justice. Second, this rising global awareness calls for greater attention to the stark inequities across countries in the standards of living and control of resources. We must not look at the welfare of U.S. citizens as the only good to be sought. Nor may we overlook the disparities of power in the relationships between this nation and the developing countries. The United States is the major supplier of food to other countries, a major source of arms sales to developing nations, and a powerful influence in multilateral institutions such as the International Monetary Fund, the World Bank, and the United Nations. What Americans see as a growing interdependence is regarded by many in the less developed countries as a pattern of domination and dependence.

14. Within this larger international setting, there are also a number of challenges to the domestic economy that call for creativity and courage. The promise of the "American dream"—freedom for all persons to develop their God-given talents to the full—remains unfulfilled for millions in the United States today.

15. Several areas of U.S. economic life demand special attention. Unemployment is the most basic. Despite the large number of new jobs the U.S. economy has generated in the past decade, approximately 8 million people seeking work in this country are unable to find it, and many more are so discouraged they have stopped looking.[8] Over the past two decades the nation has come to tolerate an increasing level of un-

---

[8] U.S. Department of Labor, Bureau of Labor Statistics, *The Employment Situation: August 1985* (September 1985), Table A-1.

employment. The 6 to 7 percent rate deemed acceptable today would have been intolerable twenty years ago. Among the unemployed are a disproportionate number of blacks, Hispanics, young people, or women who are the sole support of their families.[9] Some cities and states have many more unemployed persons than others as a result of economic forces that have little to do with people's desire to work. Unemployment is a tragedy no matter whom it strikes, but the tragedy is compounded by the unequal and unfair way it is distributed in our society.

16. Harsh poverty plagues our country despite its great wealth. More than 33 million Americans are poor; by any reasonable standard another 20 to 30 million are needy. Poverty is increasing in the United States, not decreasing.[10] For a people who believe in "progress," this should be cause for alarm. These burdens fall most heavily on blacks, Hispanics, and Native Americans. Even more disturbing is the large increase in the number of women and children living in poverty. Today children are the largest single group among the poor. This tragic fact seriously threatens the nation's future. That so many people are poor in a nation as rich as ours is a social and moral scandal that we cannot ignore.

17. Many working people and middle-class Americans live dangerously close to poverty. A rising number of families must rely on the wages of two or even three members just to get by. From 1968 to 1978 nearly a quarter of the U. S. population was in poverty part of the time and received welfare benefits in at least

---

[9] Ibid.

[10] U.S. Bureau of the Census, Current Population Reports, Series P-60, 145, *Money Income and Poverty Status of Families and Persons in the United States: 1983* (Washington, D.C.: U.S. Government Printing Office, 1984), 20.

one year.[11] The loss of a job, illness, or the breakup of a marriage may be all it takes to push people into poverty.

18. The lack of a mutually supportive relation between family life and economic life is one of the most serious problems facing the United States today.[12] The economic and cultural strength of the nation is directly linked to the stability and health of its families.[13] When families thrive, spouses contribute to the common good through their work at home, in the community, and in their jobs; and children develop a sense of their own worth and of their responsibility to serve others. When families are weak or break down entirely, the dignity of parents and children is threatened. High cultural and economic costs are inflicted on society at large.

19. The precarious economic situation of so many people and so many families calls for examination of U.S. economic arrangements. Christian conviction and the American promise of liberty and justice for all give the poor and the vulnerable a special claim on the nation's concern. They also challenge all members of the Church to help build a more just society.

20. The investment of human creativity and material resources in the production of the weapons of war makes these economic problems even more difficult to solve. Defense Department expenditures in the United States are almost $300 billion per year. The rivalry and mutual fear between superpowers divert into projects that threaten death, minds and money that could better human life. Developing countries engage in arms races they can ill afford, often with the encouragement of the superpowers. Some of the

[11] Greg H. Duncan, *Years of Poverty, Years of Plenty: The Changing Economic Fortunes of American Workers and Their Families* (Ann Arbor, Mich.: Institute for Social Research, University of Michigan, 1984).

[12] See Pope John Paul II, *Familiaris Consortio* (1981), 46.

[13] *Pastoral Constitution*, 47.

poorest countries of the world use scarce resources to buy planes, guns, and other weapons when they lack the food, education, and health care their people need. Defense policies must be evaluated and assessed in light of their real contribution to freedom, justice, and peace for the citizens of our own and other nations. We have developed a perspective on these multiple moral concerns in our 1983 pastoral letter, *The Challenge of Peace: God's Promise and Our Response*.[14] When weapons or strategies make questionable contributions to security, peace, and justice and will also be very expensive, spending priorities should be redirected to more pressing social needs.[15]

21. Many other social and economic challenges require careful analysis: the movement of many industries from the Snowbelt to the Sunbelt, the federal deficit and interest rates, corporate mergers and takeovers, the effects of new technologies such as robotics and information systems in U.S. industry, immigration policy, growing international traffic in drugs, and the trade imbalance. All of these issues do not provide a complete portrait of the economy. Rather they are symptoms of more fundamental currents shaping U.S. economic life today: the struggle to find meaning and value in human work, efforts to support individual freedom in the context of renewed social cooperation, the urgent need to create equitable forms of global interdependence in a world now marked by extreme inequality. These deeper currents are cultural and moral in content. They show that the long-range challenges facing the nation call for sustained reflection

---

[14] National Conference of Catholic Bishops, *The Challenge of Peace: God's Promise and Our Response* (Washington, D.C.: USCC Office of Publishing and Promotion Services, 1983).

[15] Cardinal Joseph L. Bernardin and Cardinal John J. O'Connor, Testimony before the House Foreign Relations Committee, June 26, 1984, *Origins* 14:10 (August 10, 1984): 157.

on the values that guide economic choices and are embodied in economic institutions. Such explicit reflection on the ethical content of economic choices and policies must become an integral part of the way Christians relate religious belief to the realities of everyday life. In this way, the "split between the faith which many profess and their daily lives,"[16] which Vatican II counted among the more serious errors of the modern age, will begin to be bridged.

C. The Need for Moral Vision

22. Sustaining a common culture and a common commitment to moral values is not easy in our world. Modern economic life is based on a division of labor into specialized jobs and professions. Since the industrial revolution, people have had to define themselves and their work ever more narrowly to find a niche in the economy. The benefits of this are evident in the satisfaction many people derive from contributing their specialized skills to society. But the costs are social fragmentation, a decline in seeing how one's work serves the whole community, and an increased emphasis on personal goals and private interests.[17] This is vividly clear in discussions of economic justice. Here it is often difficult to find a common ground among people with different backgrounds and concerns. One of our chief hopes in writing this letter is to encourage and contribute to the development of this common ground.[18]

---

[16] *Pastoral Constitution*, 43.

[17] See, for example, Peter Berger, Brigitte Berger, and Hansfried Kellner, *The Homeless Mind: Modernization and Consciousness* (New York: Vintage, 1974).

[18] For a recent study of the importance and difficulty of achieving such a common language and vision see Robert N. Bellah, Richard

23. Strengthening common moral vision is essential if the economy is to serve all people more fairly. Many middle-class Americans feel themselves in the grip of economic demands and cultural pressures that go far beyond the individual family's capacity to cope. Without constructive guidance in making decisions with serious moral implications, men and women who hold positions of responsibility in corporations or government find their duties exacting a heavy price. We want these reflections to help them contribute to a more just economy.

24. The quality of the national discussion about our economic future will affect the poor most of all, in this country and throughout the world. The life and dignity of millions of men, women, and children hang in the balance. Decisions must be judged in light of what they do *for* the poor, what they do *to* the poor, and what they enable the poor to do *for themselves*. The fundamental moral criterion for all economic decisions, policies, and institutions is this: They must be at the service of *all people, especially the poor*.

25. This letter is based on a long tradition of Catholic social thought, rooted in the Bible and developed over the past century by the popes and the Second Vatican Council in response to modern economic conditions. This tradition insists that human dignity, realized in community with others and with the whole of God's creation, is the norm against which every social institution must be measured.[19]

26. This teaching has a rich history. It is also dynamic and growing.[20] Pope Paul VI insisted that all

---

Madsen, William M. Sullivan, Ann Swidler, and Stephen M. Tipton, *Habits of the Heart: Individualism and Commitment in American Life* (Berkeley, Calif.: University of California Press, 1985). See also Martin E. Marty, *The Public Church* (New York: Crossroads, 1981).

[19] Pope John XXIII, *Mater et Magistra* (1961), 219; *Pastoral Constitution*, 40.

[20] Congregation for the Doctrine of the Faith, *Instruction on Cer-

Christian communities have the responsibility "to analyze with objectivity the situation which is proper to their own country, to shed on it the light of the Gospel's unalterable words and to draw principles of reflection, norms of judgment, and directives for action from the social teaching of the Church."[21] Therefore, we build on the past work of our own bishops' conference, including the 1919 Program of Social Reconstruction and other pastoral letters.[22] In addition many people from the Catholic, Protestant, and Jewish communities, in academic, business or political life, and from many different economic backgrounds have also provided guidance. We want to make the legacy of Christian social thought a living, growing resource that can inspire hope and help shape the future.

27. We write, then, first of all to provide guidance for members of our own Church as they seek to form their consciences about economic matters. No one may claim the name Christian and be comfortable in the face of the hunger, homelessness, insecurity, and injustice found in this country and the world. At the same time, we want to add our voice to the public debate about the directions in which the U.S. economy should be moving. We seek the cooperation and support of those who do not share our faith or tradition.

---

tain *Aspects of the Theology of Liberation* (Washington, D.C.: USCC Office of Publishing and Promotion Services, 1984); Pope Paul VI, *Octogesima Adveniens* (1971), 42.

[21] *Octogesima Adveniens*, 4.

[22] Administrative Committee of the National Catholic War Council, *Program of Social Reconstruction*, February 12, 1919. Other notable statements on the economy by our predecessors are *The Present Crisis*, April 25, 1933; *Statement on Church and Social Order*, February 4, 1940; *The Economy: Human Dimensions*, November 20, 1975. These and numerous other statements of the U.S. Catholic episcopate can be found in Hugh J. Nolan, ed., *Pastoral Letters of the United States Catholic Bishops*, 4 vols. (Washington, D.C.: USCC Office of Publishing and Promotion Services, 1984).

The common bond of humanity that links all persons is the source of our belief that the country can attain a renewed public moral vision. The questions are basic and the answers are often elusive; they challenge us to serious and sustained attention to economic justice.

Chapter II

THE CHRISTIAN VISION OF
ECONOMIC LIFE

28. The basis for all that the Church believes about
the moral dimensions of economic life is its vision of
the transcendent worth—the sacredness—of human
beings. *The dignity of the human person, realized in community with others, is the criterion against which all aspects
of economic life must be measured.*[1] All human beings,
therefore, are ends to be served by the institutions
that make up the economy, not means to be exploited
for more narrowly defined goals. Human personhood
must be respected with a reverence that is religious.
When we deal with each other, we should do so with
the sense of awe that arises in the presence of something holy and sacred. For that is what human beings
are: we are created in the image of God (Gn 1:27).
Similarly, all economic institutions must support the
bonds of community and solidarity that are essential
to the dignity of persons. Wherever our economic
arrangements fail to conform to the demands of human dignity lived in community, they must be ques-
tioned and transformed. These convictions have a
biblical basis. They are also supported by a long tradition of theological and philosophical reflection and
through the reasoned analysis of human experience
by contemporary men and women.

---

[1] *Mater et Magistra*, 219-220. See *Pastoral Constitution*, 63.

29. In presenting the Christian moral vision, we turn first to the Scriptures for guidance. Though our comments are necessarily selective, we hope that pastors and other church members will become personally engaged with the biblical texts. The Scriptures contain many passages that speak directly of economic life. We must also attend to the Bible's deeper vision of God, of the purpose of creation, and of the dignity of human life in society. Along with other churches and ecclesial communities who are "strengthened by the grace of Baptism and the hearing of God's Word," we strive to become faithful hearers and doers of the word.[2] We also claim the Hebrew Scriptures as common heritage with our Jewish brothers and sisters, and we join with them in the quest for an economic life worthy of the divine revelation we share.

A. Biblical Perspectives

30. The fundamental conviction of our faith is that human life is fulfilled in the knowledge and love of the living God in communion with others. The Sacred Scriptures offer guidance so that men and women may enter into full communion with God and with each other, and witness to God's saving acts. We discover there a God who is creator of heaven and earth, and of the human family. Though our first parents reject the God who created them, God does not abandon them, but from Abraham and Sarah forms a people of promise. When this people is enslaved in an alien land, God delivers them and makes a covenant with them in which they are summoned to be faithful to the *torah* or sacred teaching. The focal points of Israel's faith—creation, covenant, and community—provide

---

[2] Vatican Council II, *Decree on Ecumenism,* 22-23.

a foundation for reflection on issues of economic and social justice.

1. Created in God's Image

31. After the exile, when Israel combined its traditions into a written *torah*, it prefaced its history as a people with the story of the creation of all peoples and of the whole world by the same God who created them as a nation (Gn 1-11). God is the creator of heaven and earth (Gn 14:19-22; Is 40:28; 45:18); creation proclaims God's glory (Ps 89:6-12) and is "very good" (Gn 1:31). Fruitful harvests, bountiful flocks, a loving family are God's blessings on those who heed God's word. Such is the joyful refrain that echoes throughout the Bible. One legacy of this theology of creation is the conviction that no dimension of human life lies beyond God's care and concern. God is present to creation, and creative engagement with God's handiwork is itself reverence for God.

32. At the summit of creation stands the creation of man and woman, made in God's image (Gn 1:26-27). *As such every human being possesses an inalienable dignity that stamps human existence prior to any division into races or nations and prior to human labor and human achievement (Gn 4-11).* Men and women are also to share in the creative activity of God. They are to be fruitful, to care for the earth (Gn 2:15), and to have "dominion" over it (Gn 1:28), which means they are "to govern the world in holiness and justice and to render judgment in integrity of heart" (Wis 9:3). Creation is a gift; women and men are to be faithful stewards in caring for the earth. They can justly consider that by their labor they are unfolding the Creator's work.[3]

---

[3] C. Westermann, *Creation* (Philadelphia: Fortress Press, 1974); and B. Vawter, *On Genesis: A New Reading* (Garden City, N.Y.: Doubleday, 1977). See also *Pastoral Constitution*, 34.

33. The narratives of Genesis 1-11 also portray the origin of the strife and suffering that mar the world. Though created to enjoy intimacy with God and the fruits of the earth, Adam and Eve disrupted God's design by trying to live independently of God through a denial of their status as creatures. They turned away from God and gave to God's creation the obedience due to God alone. For this reason the prime sin in so much of the biblical tradition is idolatry: service of the creature rather than of the creator (Rom 1:25), and the attempt to overturn creation by making God in human likeness. The Bible castigates not only the worship of idols, but also manifestations of idolatry, such as the quest for unrestrained power and the desire for great wealth (Is 40:12-20; 44:1-20; Wis 13:1-14:31; Col 3:5, "the greed that is idolatry"). The sin of our first parents had other consequences as well. Alienation from God pits brother against brother (Gn 4:8-16), in a cycle of war and vengeance (Gn 4:22-23). Sin and evil abound, and the primeval history culminates with another assault on the heavens, this time ending in a babble of tongues scattered over the face of the earth (Gn 11:1-9). Sin simultaneously alienates human beings from God and shatters the solidarity of the human community. Yet this reign of sin is not the final word. The primeval history is followed by the call of Abraham, a man of faith, who was to be the bearer of the promise to many nations (Gn 12:1-4). Throughout the Bible we find this struggle between sin and repentance. God's judgment on evil is followed by God's seeking out a sinful people.

34. The biblical vision of creation has provided one of the most enduring legacies of Church teaching. To stand before God as the creator is to respect God's creation, both the world of nature and of human history. *From the patristic period to the present, the Church has affirmed that misuse of the world's resources or appropriation of them by a minority of the world's population*

betrays the gift of creation since "whatever belongs to God belongs to all."[4]

2. A People of the Covenant

35. When the people of Israel, our forerunners in faith, gathered in thanksgiving to renew their covenant (Jos 24:1-15), they recalled the gracious deeds of God (Dt 6:20-25; 26: 5-11). When they lived as aliens in a strange land and experienced oppression and slavery, they cried out. The Lord, the God of their ancestors, heard their cries, knew their afflictions, and came to deliver them (Ex 3:7-8). By leading them out of Egypt, God created a people that was to be the Lord's very own (Jer 24:7; Hos 2:25). They were to imitate God by treating the alien and the slave in their midst as God had treated them (Ex 22:20-22; Jer 34:8-14).

36. In the midst of this saving history stands the covenant at Sinai (Ex 19-24). It begins with an account of what God has done for the people (Ex 19:1-6; cf. Jos 24:1-13) and includes from God's side a promise of steadfast love (*hesed*) and faithfulness (*'emeth*, Ex 34:5-7). The people are summoned to ratify this covenant by faithfully worshiping God alone and by directing their lives according to God's will, which was made explicit in Israel's great legal codes such as the Decalogue (Ex 20:1-17) and the Book of the Covenant (Ex 20:22-23:33). Far from being an arbitrary restriction on the life of the people, these codes made life in

---

[4] St. Cyprian, *On Works and Almsgiving*, 25, trans. R. J. Deferrari, *St. Cyprian: Treatises*, 36 (New York: Fathers of the Church, 1958), 251. Original text in Migne, *Patrologia Latina*, vol. 4, 620. On the Patristic teaching, see C. Avila, *Ownership: Early Christian Teaching* (Maryknoll, N.Y.: Orbis Books, 1983). Collection of original texts and translations.

community possible.[5] The specific laws of the covenant protect human life and property, demand respect for parents and the spouses and children of one's neighbor, and manifest a special concern for the vulnerable members of the community: widows, orphans, the poor, and strangers in the land. Laws such as that for the Sabbath year when the land was left fallow (Ex 23:11; Lv 25:1-7) and for the year of release of debts (Dt 15:1-11) summoned people to respect the land as God's gift and reminded Israel that as a people freed by God from bondage they were to be concerned for the poor and oppressed in their midst. Every fiftieth year a jubilee was to be proclaimed as a year of "liberty throughout the land" and property was to be restored to its original owners (Lv 25:8-17, cf. Is 61:1-2; Lk 4:18-19).[6] The codes of Israel reflect the norms of the covenant: reciprocal responsibility, mercy, and truthfulness. They embody a life in freedom from oppression: worship of the One God, rejection of idolatry, mutual respect among people, care and protection for every member of the social body. Being free and being a co-responsible community are God's intentions for us.

37. When the people turn away from the living God to serve idols and no longer heed the commands of the covenant, God sends prophets to recall his saving deeds and to summon them to return to the one who betrothed them "in right and in justice, in love and in mercy" (Hos 2:21). The substance of

---

[5] T. Ogletree, *The Use of the Bible in Christian Ethics* (Philadelphia: Fortress Press, 1983), 47-85.

[6] Though scholars debate whether the Jubilee was a historical institution or an ideal, its images were continually evoked to stress God's sovereignty over the land and God's concern for the poor and the oppressed (e.g., Is 61:1-2; Lk 4:16-19). See R. North, *Sociology of the Biblical Jubilee* (Rome: Biblical Institute, 1954); S. Ringe, *Jesus, Liberation and the Biblical Jubilee: Images for Ethics and Christology* (Philadelphia: Fortress Press, 1985).

prophetic faith is proclaimed by Micah: "to do justice and to love kindness, and to walk humbly with your God" (Mi 6:8, RSV). Biblical faith in general, and prophetic faith especially, insist that fidelity to the covenant joins obedience to God with reverence and concern for the neighbor. The biblical terms which best summarize this double dimension of Israel's faith are *sedaqah*, justice (also translated as righteousness), and *mishpat* (right judgment or justice embodied in a concrete act or deed). The biblical understanding of justice gives a fundamental perspective to our reflections on social and economic justice.[7]

38. God is described as a "God of justice" (Is 30:18) who loves justice (Is 61:8, cf. Pss 11:7; 33:5; 37:28; 99:4) and delights in it (Jer 9:23). God demands justice from the whole people (Dt 16:20) and executes justice for the needy (Ps 140:13). Central to the biblical presentation of justice is that the justice of a community is measured by its treatment of the powerless in society, most often described as the widow, the orphan, the poor, and the stranger (non-Israelite) in the land. The Law, the Prophets, and the Wisdom literature of the Old Testament all show deep concern for the proper treatment of such people.[8] What these groups of people have in common is their vulnerability and lack of power. They are often alone and have no protector or advocate. Therefore, it is God who hears their cries (Pss 109:21; 113:7), and the king who is God's anointed is commanded to have special concern for them.

---

[7] On justice, see J. R. Donahue, "Biblical Perspectives on Justice," in Haughey, ed., *The Faith That Does Justice* (New York: Paulist Press, 1977), 68-112; and S. C. Mott, *Biblical Ethics and Social Change* (New York: Oxford University Press, 1982).

[8] See Ex 22:20-26; Dt 15:1-11; Jb 29:12-17; Pss 69:34; 72:2, 4, 12-24; 82:3-4; Prv 14:21, 31; Is 3:14-15; 10:2; Jer 22:16; Zec 7:9-10.

39. Justice has many nuances.[9] Fundamentally, it suggests a sense of what is right or of what should happen. For example, paths are just when they bring you to your destination (Gn 24:48; Ps 23:3), and laws are just when they create harmony within the community, as Isaiah says: "Justice will bring about peace; right will produce calm and security" (Is 32:17). God is "just" by acting as God should, coming to the people's aid and summoning them to conversion when they stray. People are summoned to be "just," that is, to be in a proper relation to God, by observing God's laws which form them into a faithful community. Biblical justice is more comprehensive than subsequent philosophical definitions. It is not concerned with a strict definition of rights and duties, but with the rightness of the human condition before God and within society. Nor is justice opposed to love; rather, it is both a manifestation of love and a condition for love to grow.[10] Because God loves Israel, he rescues them from oppression and summons them to be a people that "does justice" and loves kindness. The quest for justice arises from loving gratitude for the saving acts of God and manifests itself in wholehearted love of God and neighbor.

40. These perspectives provide the foundation for a biblical vision of economic justice. Every human person is created as an image of God, and the denial of dignity to a person is a blot on this image. Creation is a gift to all men and women, not to be appropriated for the benefit of a few; its beauty is an object of joy and reverence. The same God who came to the aid of an oppressed people and formed them into a covenant community continues to hear the cries of the

[9] J. Pedersen, *Israel: Its Life and Culture*, vol. I-II (London: Oxford University Press, 1926), 337-340.

[10] J. Alfaro, *Theology of Justice in the World* (Rome: Pontifical Commission on Justice and Peace, 1973), 40-41; E. McDonagh, *The Making of Disciples* (Wilmington, Del.: Michael Glazier, 1982), 119.

oppressed and to create communities which are responsive to God's word. God's love and life are present when people can live in a community of faith and hope. These cardinal points of the faith of Israel also furnish the religious context for understanding the saving action of God in the life and teaching of Jesus.

3. The Reign of God and Justice

41. Jesus enters human history as God's anointed son who announces the nearness of the reign of God (Mk 1:9-14). This proclamation summons us to acknowledge God as creator and covenant partner and challenges us to seek ways in which God's revelation of the dignity and destiny of all creation might become incarnate in history. It is not simply the promise of the future victory of God over sin and evil, but that this victory has already begun—in the life and teaching of Jesus.

42. What Jesus proclaims by word, he enacts in his ministry. He resists temptations of power and prestige, follows his Father's will, and teaches us to pray that it be accomplished on earth. He warns against attempts to "lay up treasures on earth" (Mt 6:19) and exhorts his followers not to be anxious about material goods but rather to seek first God's reign and God's justice (Mt 6:25-33). His mighty works symbolize that the reign of God is more powerful than evil, sickness, and the hardness of the human heart. He offers God's loving mercy to sinners (Mk 2:17), takes up the cause of those who suffered religious and social discrimination (Lk 7:36-50; 15:1-2), and attacks the use of religion to avoid the demands of charity and justice (Mk 7:9-13; Mt 23:23).

43. When asked what was the greatest commandment, Jesus quoted the age-old Jewish affirmation of faith that God alone is One and to be loved with the

whole heart, mind, and soul (Dt 6:4-5) and immediately adds: "You shall love your neighbor as yourself" (Lv 19:18, Mk 12:28-34). This dual command of love that is at the basis of all Christian morality is illustrated in the Gospel of Luke by the parable of a Samaritan who interrupts his journey to come to the aid of a dying man (Lk 10:29-37). Unlike the other wayfarers who look on the man and pass by, the Samaritan "was moved with compassion at the sight"; he stops, tends the wounded man, and takes him to a place of safety. In this parable compassion is the bridge between mere seeing and action; love is made real through effective action.[11]

44. Near the end of his life, Jesus offers a vivid picture of the last judgment (Mt 25: 31-46). All the nations of the world will be assembled and will be divided into those blessed who are welcomed into God's kingdom or those cursed who are sent to eternal punishment. The blessed are those who fed the hungry, gave drink to the thirsty, welcomed the stranger, clothed the naked, and visited the sick and imprisoned; the cursed are those who neglected these works of mercy and love. Neither the blessed nor the cursed are astounded that they are judged by the Son of Man, nor that judgment is rendered according to works of charity. The shock comes when they find that in neglecting the poor, the outcast, and the oppressed, they were rejecting Jesus himself. Jesus who came as "Emmanuel" (God with us, Mt 1:23) and who promises to be with his people until the end of the age (Mt 28:20) is hidden in those most in need; to reject them is to reject God made manifest in history.

---

[11] Pope John Paul II has drawn on this parable to exhort us to have a "compassionate heart" to those in need in his Apostolic Letter "On the Christian Meaning of Human Suffering" (*Salvifici Doloris*) (Washington, D.C.: USCC Office of Publishing and Promotion Services, 1984), 34-39.

4. Called To Be Disciples in Community

45. Jesus summoned his first followers to a change of heart and to take on the yoke of God's reign (Mk 1:14-15; Mt 11:29). They are to be the nucleus of that community which will continue the work of proclaiming and building God's kingdom through the centuries. As Jesus called the first disciples in the midst of their everyday occupations of fishing and tax collecting; so he again calls people in every age in the home, in the workplace, and in the marketplace.

46. The Church is, as Pope John Paul II reminded us, "a community of disciples" in which "we must see first and foremost Christ saying to each member of the community: follow me."[12] To be a Christian is to join with others in responding to this personal call and in learning the meaning of Christ's life. It is to be sustained by that loving intimacy with the Father that Jesus experienced in his work, in his prayer, and in his suffering.

47. Discipleship involves imitating the pattern of Jesus' life by openness to God's will in the service of others (Mk 10:42-45). Disciples are also called to follow him on the way of the cross, and to heed his call that those who lose their lives for the sake of the Gospel will save them (Mk 8:34-35). Jesus' death is an example of that greater love which lays down one's life for others (cf. Jn 15:12-18). It is a model for those who suffer persecution for the sake of justice (Mt 5:10). The death of Jesus was not the end of his power and presence, for he was raised up by the power of God. Nor did it mark the end of the disciples' union with him. After Jesus had appeared to them and when they received the gift of the Spirit (Acts 2:1-12), they became apostles of the good news to the ends of the earth. In the face of poverty and persecution they trans-

---

[12] *Redeemer of Man*, 21.

formed human lives and formed communities which became signs of the power and presence of God. Sharing in this same resurrection faith, contemporary followers of Christ can face the struggles and challenges that await those who bring the gospel vision to bear on our complex economic and social world.

5. Poverty, Riches, and the Challenge of Discipleship

48. The pattern of Christian life as presented in the Gospel of Luke has special relevance today. In her *Magnificat*, Mary rejoices in a God who scatters the proud, brings down the mighty, and raises up the poor and lowly (Lk 1:51-53). The first public utterance of Jesus is "The Spirit of the Lord is upon me, because he has anointed me to preach the good news to the poor" (Lk 4:18 cf. Is 61:1-2). Jesus adds to the blessing on the poor a warning, "Woe to you who are rich, for you have received your consolation" (Lk 6:24). He warns his followers against greed and reliance on abundant possessions and underscores this by the parable of the man whose life is snatched away at the very moment he tries to secure his wealth (Lk 12:13-21). In Luke alone, Jesus tells the parable of the rich man who does not see the poor and suffering Lazarus at his gate (Lk 16:19-31). When the rich man finally "sees" Lazarus, it is from the place of torment and the opportunity for conversion has passed. Pope John Paul II has often recalled this parable to warn the prosperous not to be blind to the great poverty that exists beside great wealth.[13]

49. Jesus, especially in Luke, lives as a poor man, like the prophets takes the side of the poor, and warns

---

[13] Address to Workers at Sao Paulo, 8, *Origins* 10:9 (July 31, 1980): 139; and Address at Yankee Stadium, *Origins* 9:19 (October 25, 1979): 311-312.

of the dangers of wealth.[14] The terms used for poor, while primarily describing lack of material goods, also suggest dependence and powerlessness. The poor are also an exiled and oppressed people whom God will rescue (Is 51:21-23) as well as a faithful remnant who take refuge in God (Zep 3:12-13). Throughout the Bible, material poverty is a misfortune and a cause of sadness. A constant biblical refrain is that the poor must be cared for and protected and that when they are exploited, God hears their cries (Prv 22:22-23). Conversely, even though the goods of the earth are to be enjoyed and people are to thank God for material blessings, wealth is a constant danger. The rich are wise in their own eyes (Prv 28:11), and are prone to apostasy and idolatry (Am 5:4-13; Is 2:6-8), as well as to violence and oppression (Jas 2:6-7).[15] Since they are neither blinded by wealth nor make it into an idol, the poor can be open to God's presence; throughout Israel's history and in early Christianity the poor are agents of God's transforming power.

50. The poor are often related to the lowly (Mt 5:3,5) to whom God reveals what was hidden from the wise (Mt 11:25-30). When Jesus calls the poor "blessed," he is not praising their condition of poverty, but their openness to God. When he states that the reign of God is theirs, he voices God's special concern for them, and promises that they are to be the beneficiaries of God's mercy and justice. When he summons disciples to leave all and follow him, he

---

[14] J. Dupont and A. George, eds., *La pauvrete evangelique* (Paris: Cerf, 1971); M. Hengel, *Property and Riches in the Early Church* (Philadelphia: Fortress Press, 1974); L. Johnson, *Sharing Possessions: Mandate and Symbol of Faith* (Philadelphia: Fortress Press, 1981); D. L. Mealand, *Poverty and Expectation in the Gospels* (London: SPCK, 1980); W. Pilgrim, *Good News to the Poor: Wealth and Poverty in Luke-Acts* (Minneapolis: Augsburg, 1981); and W. Stegemann, *The Gospel and the Poor* (Philadelphia: Fortress Press, 1984).

[15] See Am 4:1-3; Jb 20:19; Sir 13:4-7; Jas 2:6; 5:1-6; Rv 18:11-19.

is calling them to share his own radical trust in the Father and his freedom from care and anxiety (cf. Mt 6:25-34). The practice of evangelical poverty in the Church has always been a living witness to the power of that trust and to the joy that comes with that freedom.

51. Early Christianity saw the poor as an object of God's special love, but it neither canonized material poverty nor accepted deprivation as an inevitable fact of life. Though few early Christians possessed wealth or power (1 Cor 1:26-28; Jas 2:5), their communities had well-off members (Acts 16:14; 18:8). Jesus' concern for the poor was continued in different forms in the early Church. The early community at Jerusalem distributed its possessions so that "there was no needy person among them," and held "all things in common"—a phrase that suggests not only shared material possessions, but more fundamentally, friendship and mutual concern among all its members (Acts 4:32-34; 2:44). While recognizing the dangers of wealth, the early Church proposed the proper use of possessions to alleviate need and suffering, rather than universal dispossession. Beginning in the first century and throughout history, Christian communities have developed varied structures to support and sustain the weak and powerless in societies that were often brutally unconcerned about human suffering.

52. Such perspectives provide a basis today for what is called the "preferential option for the poor."[16] Though in the Gospels and in the New Testament as a whole the offer of salvation is extended to all peoples, Jesus takes the side of those most in need, physically and spiritually. The example of Jesus poses a number of challenges to the contemporary Church. It imposes a prophetic mandate to speak for those who have no one to speak for them, to be a defender

---

[16] See paras. 85-91.

of the defenseless, who in biblical terms are the poor. It also demands a compassionate vision that enables the Church to see things from the side of the poor and powerless and to assess lifestyle, policies, and social institutions in terms of their impact on the poor. It summons the Church also to be an instrument in assisting people to experience the liberating power of God in their own lives so that they may respond to the Gospel in freedom and in dignity. Finally, and most radically, it calls for an emptying of self, both individually and corporately, that allows the Church to experience the power of God in the midst of poverty and powerlessness.

6. A Community of Hope

53. The biblical vision of creation, covenant, and community, as well as the summons to discipleship, unfolds under the tension between promise and fulfillment. The whole Bible is spanned by the narratives of the first creation (Gn 1-3) and the vision of a restored creation at the end of history (Rv 21:1-4). Just as creation tells us that God's desire was one of wholeness and unity between God and the human family and within this family itself, the images of a new creation give hope that enmity and hatred will cease and justice and peace will reign (Is 11:4-6; 25:l-8). Human life unfolds "between the times," the time of the first creation and that of a restored creation (Rom 8:18-25). Although the ultimate realization of God's plan lies in the future, Christians in union with all people of good will are summoned to shape history in the image of God's creative design, and in response to the reign of God proclaimed and embodied by Jesus.

54. A Christian is a member of a new community, "God's own people" (1 Pt 2:9-10), who, like the people of Exodus, owes its existence to the gracious gift of God and is summoned to respond to God's will made

manifest in the life and teaching of Jesus. A Christian walks in the newness of life (Rom 6:4), and is "a new creation; the old has passed away, the new has come" (2 Cor 5:17). This new creation in Christ proclaims that God's creative love is constantly at work, offers sinners forgiveness, and reconciles a broken world. Our action on behalf of justice in our world proceeds from the conviction that, despite the power of injustice and violence, life has been fundamentally changed by the entry of the Word made flesh into human history.

55. Christian communities that commit themselves to solidarity with those suffering and to confrontation with those attitudes and ways of acting which institutionalize injustice, will themselves experience the power and presence of Christ. They will embody in their lives the values of the new creation while they labor under the old. The quest for economic and social justice will always combine hope and realism, and must be renewed by every generation. It involves diagnosing those situations that continue to alienate the world from God's creative love as well as presenting hopeful alternatives that arise from living in a renewed creation. This quest arises from faith and is sustained by hope as it seeks to speak to a broken world of God's justice and loving kindness.

7. A Living Tradition

56. Our reflection on U.S. economic life today must be rooted in this biblical vision of the kingdom and discipleship, but it must also be shaped by the rich and complex tradition of Catholic life and thought. Throughout its history, the Christian community has listened to the words of Scripture and sought to enact them in the midst of daily life in very different historical and cultural contexts.

57. In the first centuries, when Christians were a minority in a hostile society, they cared for one an-

other through generous almsgiving. In the patristic era, the church fathers repeatedly stressed that the goods of the earth were created by God for the benefit of every person without exception, and that all have special duties toward those in need. The monasteries of the Middle Ages were centers of prayer, learning, and education. They contributed greatly to the cultural and economic life of the towns and cities that sprang up around them. In the twelfth century the new mendicant orders dedicated themselves to following Christ in poverty and to the proclamation of the good news to the poor.

58. These same religious communities also nurtured some of the greatest theologians of the Church's tradition, thinkers who synthesized the call of Christ with the philosophical learning of Greek, Roman, Jewish, and Arab worlds. Thomas Aquinas and the other scholastics devoted rigorous intellectual energy to clarifying the meaning of both personal virtue and justice in society. In more recent centuries Christians began to build a large network of hospitals, orphanages, and schools, to serve the poor and society at large. And beginning with Leo XIII's *Rerum Novarum*, down to the writings and speeches of John Paul II, the popes have more systematically addressed the rapid change of modern society in a series of social encyclicals. These teachings of modern popes and of the Second Vatican Council are especially significant for efforts to respond to the problems facing society today.[17]

59. We also have much to learn from the strong emphasis in Protestant traditions on the vocation of lay people in the world and from ecumenical efforts to develop an economic ethic that addresses newly emergent problems. And in a special way our fellow Catholics in developing countries have much to teach

---

[17] See Selected Bibliography.

us about the Christian response to an ever more interdependent world.

60. Christians today are called by God to carry on this tradition through active love of neighbor, a love that responds to the special challenges of this moment in human history. The world is wounded by sin and injustice, in need of conversion and of the transformation that comes when persons enter more deeply into the mystery of the death and Resurrection of Christ. The concerns of this pastoral letter are not at all peripheral to the central mystery at the heart of the Church.[18] They are integral to the proclamation of the Gospel and part of the vocation of every Christian today.[19]

B. Ethical Norms for Economic Life

61. These biblical and theological themes shape the overall Christian perspective on economic ethics. This perspective is also subscribed to by many who do not share Christian religious convictions. Human understanding and religious belief are complementary, not contradictory. For human beings are created in God's image, and their dignity is manifest in the ability to reason and understand, in their freedom to shape their own lives and the life of their communities, and in the capacity for love and friendship. In proposing ethical norms, therefore, we appeal both to Christians and to all in our pluralist society to show that respect and reverence owed to the dignity of every person. Intelligent reflection on the social and economic realities of today is also indispensable in the effort to

---

[18] Extraordinary Synod of Bishops (1985) *The Final Report*, II, A (Washington, D.C.: USCC Office of Publishing and Promotion Services, 1986).

[19] Pope Paul VI, *On Evangelization in the Modern World*, 31.

respond to economic circumstances never envisioned in biblical times. Therefore, we now want to propose an ethical framework that can guide economic life today in ways that are both faithful to the Gospel and shaped by human experience and reason.

62. First we outline the *duties* all people have to each other and to the whole community: love of neighbor, the basic requirements of justice, and the special obligation to those who are poor or vulnerable. Corresponding to these duties are the *human rights* of every person; the obligation to protect the dignity of all demands respect for these rights. Finally these duties and rights entail several *priorities* that should guide the economic choices of individuals, communities, and the nation as a whole.

1. The Responsibilities of Social Living

63. Human life is life in community. Catholic social teaching proposes several complementary perspectives that show how moral responsibilities and duties in the economic sphere are rooted in this call to community.

a. Love and Solidarity

64. *The commandments to love God with all one's heart and to love one's neighbor as oneself are the heart and soul of Christian morality.* Jesus offers himself as the model of this all-inclusive love: ". . . love one another as I have loved you" (Jn 15:12). These commands point out the path toward true human fulfillment and happiness. They are not arbitrary restrictions on human freedom. Only active love of God and neighbor makes the fullness of community happen. Christians look forward in hope to a true communion among all persons with each other and with God. The Spirit of

Christ labors in history to build up the bonds of solidarity among all persons until that day on which their union is brought to perfection in the Kingdom of God.[20] Indeed Christian theological reflection on the very reality of God as a trinitarian unity of persons—Father, Son, and Holy Spirit—shows that being a person means being united to other persons in mutual love.[21]

65. What the Bible and Christian tradition teach, human wisdom confirms. Centuries before Christ, the Greeks and Romans spoke of the human person as a "social animal" made for friendship, community, and public life. These insights show that human beings achieve self-realization not in isolation, but in interaction with others.[22]

66. The virtues of citizenship are an expression of Christian love more crucial in today's interdependent world than ever before. These virtues grow out of a lively sense of one's dependence on the commonweal and obligations to it. This civic commitment must also guide the economic institutions of society. In the absence of a vital sense of citizenship among the businesses, corporations, labor unions, and other groups that shape economic life, society as a whole is endangered. Solidarity is another name for this social friendship and civic commitment that make human moral and economic life possible.

67. The Christian tradition recognizes, of course, that the fullness of love and community will be achieved only when God's work in Christ comes to completion in the kingdom of God. This kingdom has been inaugurated among us, but God's redeeming and transforming work is not yet complete. Within history, knowledge of how to achieve the goal of social unity is limited. Human sin continues to wound the

---

[20] Ibid., 24.
[21] *Pastoral Constitution*, 32.
[22] Ibid., 25.

lives of both individuals and larger social bodies and places obstacles in the path toward greater social solidarity. If efforts to protect human dignity are to be effective, they must take these limits on knowledge and love into account. Nevertheless, sober realism should not be confused with resigned or cynical pessimism. It is a challenge to develop a courageous hope that can sustain efforts that will sometimes be arduous and protracted.

b. Justice and Participation

68. Biblical justice is the goal we strive for. This rich biblical understanding portrays a just society as one marked by the fullness of love, compassion, holiness, and peace. On their path through history, however, sinful human beings need more specific guidance on how to move toward the realization of this great vision of God's Kingdom. This guidance is contained in the norms of basic or minimal justice. These norms state the *minimum* levels of mutual care and respect that all persons owe to each other in an imperfect world.[23] Catholic social teaching, like much philosophical reflection, distinguishes three dimensions of basic justice: commutative justice, distributive justice, and social justice.[24]

69. *Commutative justice calls for fundamental fairness in all agreements and exchanges between individuals or private social groups.* It demands respect for the equal human dignity of all persons in economic transactions, contracts, or promises. For example, workers owe their employers diligent work in exchange for

[23] See para. 39.
[24] Josef Pieper, *The Four Cardinal Virtues* (Notre Dame, Ind.: University of Notre Dame Press, 1966), 43-116; David Hollenbach, "Modern Catholic Teachings concerning Justice," in John C. Haughey ed., *The Faith That Does Justice* (New York: Paulist Press, 1977), 207-231.

their wages. Employers are obligated to treat their employees as persons, paying them fair wages in exchange for the work done and establishing conditions and patterns of work that are truly human.[25]

70. *Distributive justice requires that the allocation of income, wealth, and power in society be evaluated in light of its effects on persons whose basic material needs are unmet.* The Second Vatican Council stated: "The right to have a share of earthly goods sufficient for oneself and one's family belongs to everyone. The fathers and doctors of the Church held this view, teaching that we are obliged to come to the relief of the poor and to do so not merely out of our superfluous goods."[26] Minimum material resources are an absolute necessity for human life. If persons are to be recognized as members of the human community, then the community has an obligation to help fulfill these basic needs unless an absolute scarcity of resources makes this strictly impossible. No such scarcity exists in the United States today.

71. Justice also has implications for the way the larger social, economic, and political institutions of society are organized. *Social justice implies that persons have an obligation to be active and productive participants in the life of society and that society has a duty to enable them to participate in this way.* This form of justice can also be called "contributive," for it stresses the duty of all who are able to help create the goods, services, and other nonmaterial or spiritual values necessary for the welfare of the whole community. In the words of Pius XI, "It is of the very essence of social justice to demand from each individual all that is necessary

---

[25] Jon P. Gunnemann, "Capitalism and Commutative Justice," presented at the 1985 meeting of the Society of Christian Ethics, forthcoming in *The Annual of the Society of Christian Ethics*.

[26] *Pastoral Constitution,* 69.

for the common good."[27] Productivity is essential if the community is to have the resources to serve the well-being of all. Productivity, however, cannot be measured solely by its output in goods and services. Patterns of production must also be measured in light of their impact on the fulfillment of basic needs, employment levels, patterns of discrimination, environmental quality, and sense of community.

72. The meaning of social justice also includes a duty to organize economic and social institutions so that people can contribute to society in ways that respect their freedom and the dignity of their labor. Work should enable the working person to become "more a human being," more capable of acting intelligently, freely, and in ways that lead to self-realization.[28]

73. Economic conditions that leave large numbers of able people unemployed, underemployed, or employed in dehumanizing conditions fail to meet the converging demands of these three forms of basic justice. Work with adequate pay for all who seek it is the primary means for achieving basic justice in our society. Discrimination in job opportunities or income levels on the basis of race, sex, or other arbitrary standards can never be justified.[29] It is a scandal that such discrimination continues in the United States today. Where the effects of past discrimination persist, society has the obligation to take positive steps to overcome the legacy of injustice. Judiciously administered affirmative action programs in education and em-

---

[27] Pope Pius XI, *Divini Redemptoris*, 51. See John A. Ryan, *Distributive Justice*, third edition (New York: Macmillan, 1942), 188. The term "social justice" has been used in several different but related ways in the Catholic ethical tradition. See William Ferree, "The Act of Social Justice," *Philosophical Studies*, vol. 72 (Washington, D.C.: The Catholic University of America Press, 1943).

[28] *On Human Work*, 6, 9.

[29] *Pastoral Constitution*, 29.

ployment can be important expressions of the drive for solidarity and participation that is at the heart of true justice. Social harm calls for social relief.

74. Basic justice also calls for the establishment of a floor of material well-being on which all can stand. This is a duty of the whole of society and it creates particular obligations for those with greater resources. This duty calls into question extreme inequalities of income and consumption when so many lack basic necessities. Catholic social teaching does not maintain that a flat, arithmetical equality of income and wealth is a demand of justice, but it does challenge economic arrangements that leave large numbers of people impoverished. Further, it sees extreme inequality as a threat to the solidarity of the human community, for great disparities lead to deep social divisions and conflict.[30]

75. This means that all of us must examine our way of living in light of the needs of the poor. Christian faith and the norms of justice impose distinct limits on what we consume and how we view material goods. The great wealth of the United States can easily blind us to the poverty that exists in this nation and the destitution of hundreds of millions of people in other parts of the world. Americans are challenged today as never before to develop the inner freedom to resist the temptation constantly to seek more. Only in this way will the nation avoid what Paul VI called "the most evident form of moral underdevelopment," namely greed.[31]

76. These duties call not only for individual charitable giving but also for a more systematic approach by businesses, labor unions, and the many other groups that shape economic life—as well as government. The concentration of privilege that exists today

---

[30] Ibid. See below, paras. 180-182.
[31] Pope Paul VI, *On the Development of Peoples* (1967), 19.

results far more from institutional relationships that distribute power and wealth inequitably than from differences in talent or lack of desire to work. These institutional patterns must be examined and revised if we are to meet the demands of basic justice. For example, a system of taxation based on assessment according to ability to pay[32] is a prime necessity for the fulfillment of these social obligations.

c. Overcoming Marginalization and Powerlessness

77. These fundamental duties can be summarized this way: *Basic justice demands the establishment of minimum levels of participation in the life of the human community for all persons.* The ultimate injustice is for a person or group to be treated actively or abandoned passively as if they were nonmembers of the human race. To treat people this way is effectively to say that they simply do not count as human beings. This can take many forms, all of which can be described as varieties of marginalization, or exclusion from social life.[33] This exclusion can occur in the political sphere: restriction of free speech, concentration of power in the hands of a few, or outright repression by the state. It can also take economic forms that are equally harmful. Within the United States, individuals, families, and local communities fall victim to a downward cycle of poverty generated by economic forces they are powerless to influence. The poor, the disabled, and the unemployed too often are simply left behind. This pattern is even more severe beyond our borders in the least-developed countries. Whole nations are prevented from fully participating in the international economic order because they lack the power to change

---

[32] *Mater et Magistra*, 132.
[33] *Justice in the World*, 10, 16; and *Octogesima Adveniens*, 15.

their disadvantaged position. Many people within the less developed countries are excluded from sharing in the meager resources available in their homelands by unjust elites and unjust governments. These patterns of exclusion are created by free human beings. In this sense they can be called forms of social sin.[34] Acquiescence in them or failure to correct them when it is possible to do so is a sinful dereliction of Christian duty.

78. Recent Catholic social thought regards the task of overcoming these patterns of exclusion and powerlessness as a most basic demand of justice. Stated positively, justice demands that social institutions be ordered in a way that guarantees all persons the ability to participate actively in the economic, political, and cultural life of society.[35] The level of participation may legitimately be greater for some persons than for others, but there is a basic level of access that must be made available for all. Such participation is an essential expression of the social nature of human beings and of their communitarian vocation.

2. Human Rights: The Minimum Conditions for Life in Community

79. Catholic social teaching spells out the basic demands of justice in greater detail in the human rights of every person. These fundamental rights are prerequisites for a dignified life in community. The Bible vigorously affirms the sacredness of every person as

[34] *Pastoral Constitution*, 25; *Justice in the World*, 51; Pope John Paul II, *The Gift of the Redemption* Apostolic Exhortation on Reconciliation and Penance (Washington, D.C: USCC Office of Publishing and Promotion Services, 1984), 16; Congregation for the Doctrine of the Faith, *Instruction on Christian Freedom and Liberation*, 42, 74.

[35] In the words of the 1971 Synod of Bishops: "Participation constitutes a right which is to be applied in the economic and in the social and political field," *Justice in the World*, 18.

a creature formed in the image and likeness of God. The biblical emphasis on covenant and community also shows that human dignity can only be realized and protected in solidarity with others. In Catholic social thought, therefore, respect for human rights and a strong sense of both personal and community responsibility are linked, not opposed. Vatican II described the common good as "the sum of those conditions of social life which allow social groups and their individual members relatively thorough and ready access to their own fulfillment."[36] These conditions include the rights to fulfillment of material needs, a guarantee of fundamental freedoms, and the protection of relationships that are essential to participation in the life of society.[37] These rights are bestowed on human beings by God and grounded in the nature and dignity of human persons. They are not created by society. Indeed society has a duty to secure and protect them.[38]

80. The full range of human rights has been systematically outlined by John XXIII in his encyclical *Peace on Earth*. His discussion echoes the United Nations Universal Declaration of Human Rights and implies that internationally accepted human rights standards are strongly supported by Catholic teaching. These rights include the civil and political rights to freedom of speech, worship, and assembly. A number of human rights also concern human welfare and are of a specifically economic nature. First among these are the rights to life, food, clothing, shelter, rest, medical care, and basic education. These are indispensable to the protection of human dignity. In order to ensure

---

[36] *Pastoral Constitution*, 26.

[37] Pope John Paul II, Address at the General Assembly of the United Nations (October 2, 1979), 13, 14.

[38] See Pope Pius XII, 1941 Pentecost Address, in V. Yzermans, *The Major Addresses of Pope Pius XII*, vol. I (St. Paul: North Central, 1961), 32-33.

these necessities, all persons have a right to earn a living, which for most people in our economy is through remunerative employment. All persons also have a right to security in the event of sickness, unemployment, and old age. Participation in the life of the community calls for the protection of this same right to employment, as well as the right to healthful working conditions, to wages, and other benefits sufficient to provide individuals and their families with a standard of living in keeping with human dignity, and to the possibility of property ownership.[39] These fundamental personal rights—civil and political as well as social and economic—state the minimum conditions for social institutions that respect human dignity, social solidarity, and justice. They are all essential to human dignity and to the integral development of both individuals and society, and are thus moral issues.[40] Any denial of these rights harms persons and wounds the human community. Their serious and sustained denial violates individuals and destroys solidarity among persons.

81. Social and economic rights call for a mode of implementation different from that required to secure civil and political rights. Freedom of worship and of speech imply immunity from interference on the part of both other persons and the government. The rights

---

[39] *Peace on Earth,* 8-27. See *On Human Work,* 18-19. *Peace on Earth* and other modern papal statements refer explicitly to the "right to work" as one of the fundamental economic rights. Because of the ambiguous meaning of the phrase in the United States, and also because the ordinary way people earn their living in our society is through paid employment, the NCCB has affirmed previously that the protection of human dignity demands that the right to useful employment be secured for all who are able and willing to work. See NCCB, *The Economy: Human Dimensions* (November 20, 1975), 5, in NCCB, *Justice in the Marketplace,* 470. See also Congregation for the Doctrine of the Faith, *Instruction on Christian Freedom and Liberation,* 85.

[40] *The Development of Peoples,* 14.

to education, employment, and social security, for example, are empowerments that call for positive action by individuals and society at large.

82. However, both kinds of rights call for positive action to create social and political institutions that enable all persons to become active members of society. Civil and political rights allow persons to participate freely in the public life of the community, for example, through free speech, assembly, and the vote. In democratic countries these rights have been secured through a long and vigorous history of creating the institutions of constitutional government. In seeking to secure the full range of social and economic rights today, a similar effort to shape new economic arrangements will be necessary.

83. The first step in such an effort is the development of a new cultural consensus that the basic economic conditions of human welfare are essential to human dignity and are due persons by right. Second, the securing of these rights will make demands on *all* members of society, on all private sector institutions, and on government. A concerted effort on all levels in our society is needed to meet these basic demands of justice and solidarity. Indeed political democracy and a commitment to secure economic rights are mutually reinforcing.

84. Securing economic rights for all will be an arduous task. There are a number of precedents in U.S. history, however, which show that the work has already begun.[41] The country needs a serious dialogue about the appropriate levels of private and public sector involvement that are needed to move forward. There is certainly room for diversity of opinion in the Church and in U.S. society on *how* to protect the hu-

---

[41] Martha H. Good, "Freedom from Want: The Failure of United States Courts to Protect Subsistence Rights," *Human Rights Quarterly* 6 (1984): 335-365.

man dignity and economic rights of all our brothers and sisters.[42] In our view, however, there can be no legitimate disagreement on the basic moral objectives.

3. Moral Priorities for the Nation

85. *The common good demands justice for all, the protection of the human rights of all.*[43] Making cultural and economic institutions more supportive of the freedom, power, and security of individuals and families must be a central, long-range objective for the nation. Every person has a duty to contribute to building up the commonweal. All have a responsibility to develop their talents through education. Adults must contribute to society through their individual vocations and talents. Parents are called to guide their children to the maturity of Christian adulthood and responsible citizenship. Everyone has special duties toward the poor and the marginalized. Living up to these responsibilities, however, is often made difficult by the social and economic patterns of society. Schools and educational policies both public and private often serve the privileged exceedingly well, while the children of the poor are effectively abandoned as second-class citizens. Great stresses are created in family life by the way work is organized and scheduled, and by the social and cultural values communicated on TV. Many in the lower middle class are barely getting by and fear becoming victims of economic forces over which they have no control.

86. *The obligation to provide justice for all means that the poor have the single most urgent economic claim on the conscience of the nation.* Poverty can take many forms, spiritual as well as material. All people face struggles of the spirit as they ask deep questions about their

---

[42] *Pastoral Constitution,* 43.
[43] *Mater et Magistra,* 65.

purpose in life. Many have serious problems in marriage and family life at some time in their lives, and all of us face the certain reality of sickness and death. The Gospel of Christ proclaims that God's love is stronger than all these forms of diminishment. Material deprivation, however, seriously compounds such sufferings of the spirit and heart. To see a loved one sick is bad enough, but to have no possibility of obtaining health care is worse. To face family problems, such as the death of a spouse or a divorce, can be devastating, but to have these lead to the loss of one's home and end with living on the streets is something no one should have to endure in a country as rich as ours. In developing countries these human problems are even more greatly intensified by extreme material deprivation. This form of human suffering can be reduced if our own country, so rich in resources, chooses to increase its assistance.

87. As individuals and as a nation, therefore, we are called to make a fundamental "option for the poor."[44] The obligation to evaluate social and economic activity from the viewpoint of the poor and the powerless arises from the radical command to love one's neighbor as one's self. Those who are marginalized and whose rights are denied have privileged claims if society is to provide justice for *all*. This obligation is deeply rooted in Christian belief. As Paul VI stated:

---

[44] On the recent use of this term see: Congregation for the Doctrine of the Faith, *Instruction on Christian Freedom and Liberation*, 46-50, 66-68; *Evangelization in Latin America's Present and Future*, Final Document of the Third General Conference of the Latin American Episcopate (Puebla, Mexico, January 27-February 13, 1979), esp. part VI, ch. 1, "A Preferential Option for the Poor," in J. Eagleson and P. Scharper, eds., *Puebla and Beyond* (Maryknoll: Orbis Books, 1979), 264-267; Donal Dorr, *Option for the Poor: A Hundred Years of Vatican Social Teaching* (Dublin: Gill and Macmillan/Maryknoll, N.Y.: Orbis Books, 1983).

> In teaching us charity, the Gospel instructs us in the
> preferential respect due the poor and the special sit-
> uation they have in society: the more fortunate should
> renounce some of their rights so as to place their goods
> more generously at the service of others.[45]

John Paul II has described this special obligation to
the poor as "a call to have a special openness with
the small and the weak, those that suffer and weep,
those that are humiliated and left on the margin of
society, so as to help them win their dignity as human
persons and children of God."[46]

88. The prime purpose of this special commitment
to the poor is to enable them to become active participants in the life of society. It is to enable *all* persons
to share in and contribute to the common good.[47] The
"option for the poor," therefore, is not an adversarial
slogan that pits one group or class against another.
Rather it states that the deprivation and powerlessness of the poor wounds the whole community. The
extent of their suffering is a measure of how far we
are from being a true community of persons. These
wounds will be healed only by greater solidarity with
the poor and among the poor themselves.

89. In summary, the norms of love, basic justice,
and human rights imply that personal decisions, social
policies, and economic institutions should be governed by several key priorities. These priorities do not
specify everything that must be considered in economic decision making. They do indicate the most
fundamental and urgent objectives.

90. a. *The fulfillment of the basic needs of the poor is of
the highest priority.* Personal decisions, policies of pri-

---

[45] *Octogesima Adveniens,* 23.

[46] Address to Bishops of Brazil, 6, 9, *Origins* 10:9 (July 31, 1980):
135.

[47] Pope John Paul II, Address to Workers at Sao Paulo, 4, *Origins,*
10:9 (July 31, 1980): 138; Congregation for the Doctrine of the Faith,
Instruction on Christian Freedom and Liberation, 66-68.

vate and public bodies, and power relationships must all be evaluated by their effects on those who lack the minimum necessities of nutrition, housing, education, and health care. In particular, this principle recognizes that meeting fundamental human needs must come before the fulfillment of desires for luxury consumer goods, for profits not conducive to the common good, and for unnecessary military hardware.

91. b. *Increasing active participation in economic life by those who are presently excluded or vulnerable is a high social priority.* The human dignity of all is realized when people gain the power to work together to improve their lives, strengthen their families, and contribute to society. Basic justice calls for more than providing help to the poor and other vulnerable members of society. It recognizes the priority of policies and programs that support family life and enhance economic participation through employment and widespread ownership of property. It challenges privileged economic power in favor of the well-being of all. It points to the need to improve the present situation of those unjustly discriminated against in the past. And it has very important implications for both the domestic and the international distribution of power.

92. c. *The investment of wealth, talent, and human energy should be specially directed to benefit those who are poor or economically insecure.* Achieving a more just economy in the United States and the world depends in part on increasing economic resources and productivity. In addition, the ways these resources are invested and managed must be scrutinized in light of their effects on non-monetary values. Investment and management decisions have crucial moral dimensions: they create jobs or eliminate them; they can push vulnerable families over the edge into poverty or give them new hope for the future; they help or hinder the building of a more equitable society. Indeed

they can have either positive or negative influence on the fairness of the global economy. Therefore, this priority presents a strong moral challenge to policies that put large amounts of talent and capital into the production of luxury consumer goods and military technology while failing to invest sufficiently in education, health, the basic infrastructure of our society, and economic sectors that produce urgently needed jobs, goods, and services.

93. d. *Economic and social policies as well as the organization of the work world should be continually evaluated in light of their impact on the strength and stability of family life.* The long-range future of this nation is intimately linked with the well-being of families, for the family is the most basic form of human community.[48] Efficiency and competition in the marketplace must be moderated by greater concern for the way work schedules and compensation support or threaten the bonds between spouses and between parents and children. Health, education, and social service programs should be scrutinized in light of how well they ensure both individual dignity and family integrity.

94. These priorities are not policies. They are norms that should guide the economic choices of all and shape economic institutions. They can help the United States move forward to fulfill the duties of justice and protect economic rights. They were strongly affirmed as implications of Catholic social teaching by Pope John Paul II during his visit to Canada in 1984: "The needs of the poor take priority over the desires of the rich; the rights of workers over the maximization of profits; the preservation of the environment over uncontrolled industrial expansion; production to meet social needs over production for military purposes."[49]

---

[48] *Pastoral Constitution*, 47.

[49] Address on Christian Unity in a Technological Age (Toronto, September 14, 1984) in *Origins* 14:16 (October 4, 1984): 248.

There will undoubtedly be disputes about the concrete applications of these priorities in our complex world. We do not seek to foreclose discussion about them. However, we believe that an effort to move in the direction they indicate is urgently needed.

95. The economic challenge of today has many parallels with the political challenge that confronted the founders of our nation. In order to create a new form of political democracy they were compelled to develop ways of thinking and political institutions that had never existed before. Their efforts were arduous and their goals imperfectly realized, but they launched an experiment in the protection of civil and political rights that has prospered through the efforts of those who came after them. *We believe the time has come for a similar experiment in securing economic rights: the creation of an order that guarantees the minimum conditions of human dignity in the economic sphere for every person.* By drawing on the resources of the Catholic moral-religious tradition, we hope to make a contribution through this letter to such a new "American Experiment": a new venture to secure economic justice for all.

C. Working for Greater Justice: Persons and Institutions

96. The economy of this nation has been built by the labor of human hands and minds. Its future will be forged by the ways persons direct all this work toward greater justice. The economy is not a machine that operates according to its own inexorable laws, and persons are not mere objects tossed about by economic forces. Pope John Paul II has stated that "human work is a key, probably the essential key, to the whole social question."[50] The Pope's understand-

---

[50] *On Human Work,* 3.

ing of work includes virtually all forms of productive human activity: agriculture, entrepreneurship, industry, the care of children, the sustaining of family life, politics, medical care, and scientific research. Leisure, prayer, celebration, and the arts are also central to the realization of human dignity and to the development of a rich cultural life. It is in their daily work, however, that persons become the subjects and creators of the economic life of the nation.[51] Thus, it is primarily through their daily labor that people make their most important contributions to economic justice.

97. All work has a threefold moral significance. First, it is a principal way that people exercise the distinctive human capacity for self-expression and self-realization. Second, it is the ordinary way for human beings to fulfill their material needs. Finally, work enables people to contribute to the well-being of the larger community. Work is not only for one's self. It is for one's family, for the nation, and indeed for the benefit of the entire human family.[52]

98. These three moral concerns should be visible in the work of all, no matter what their role in the economy: blue collar workers, managers, homemakers, politicians, and others. They should also govern the activities of the many different, overlapping communities and institutions that make up society: families, neighborhoods, small businesses, giant corporations, trade unions, the various levels of government, international organizations, and a host of other human associations including communities of faith.

99. Catholic social teaching calls for respect for the full richness of social life. The need for vital contributions from different human associations—ranging

---

[51] Ibid., 5, 6.
[52] Ibid., 6, 10.

in size from the family to government—has been classically expressed in Catholic social teaching in the "principle of subsidiarity":

> Just as it is gravely wrong to take from individuals what they can accomplish by their own initiative and industry and give it to the community, so also it is an injustice and at the same time a grave evil and disturbance of right order to assign to a greater and higher association what lesser and subordinate organizations can do. For every social activity ought of its very nature to furnish help (*subsidium*) to the members of the body social, and never destroy and absorb them.[53]

100. This principle guarantees institutional pluralism. It provides space for freedom, initiative, and creativity on the part of many social agents. At the same time, it insists that *all* these agents should work in ways that help build up the social body. Therefore, in all their activities these groups should be working in ways that express their distinctive capacities for action, that help meet human needs, and that make

---

[53] *Quadragesimo Anno*, 79. The meaning of this principle is not always accurately understood. For studies of its interpretation in Catholic teaching see: Calvez and Perrin in John F. Cronin, *Catholic Social Principles*, (Milwaukee: Bruce, 1950), 328-342; Johannes Messner, "Freedom as a Principle of Social Order: An Essay in the Substance of Subsidiary Function," *Modern Schoolman* 28 (1951): 97-110; Richard E. Mulcahy, "Subsidiarity," *New Catholic Encyclopedia* vol. 13 (New York: McGraw-Hill, 1966), 762; Franz H. Mueller, "The Principle of Subsidiarity in Christian Tradition," *American Catholic Sociological Review* 4 (October 1943): 144-157; Oswald von Nell-Breuning, "Zur Sozialreform, Erwagungen zum Subsidiaritatsprinzip," *Stimmen der Zeit* 157, Bd. 81 (1955-1956): 1-11; id., "Subsidiarity," *Sacramentum Mundi*, vol. 6 (New York: Herder and Herder, 1970), 6, 114-116; Arthur Fridolin Utz, *Formen und Grenzen des Subsidiaritatsprinzips* (Heidelberg: F. H. Kerle Verlag, 1956); id., "The Principle of Subsidiarity and Contemporary Natural Law," *Natural Law Forum* 3 (1958): 170-183; id., *Grundsatze der Sozialpolitik: Solidaritat und Subsidiaritat in der Alterversicherung* (Stuttgart: Sewald Verlag, 1969).

true contributions to the common good of the human community. The task of creating a more just U.S. economy is the vocation of all and depends on strengthening the virtues of public service and responsible citizenship in personal life and on all levels of institutional life.[54]

101. Without attempting to describe the tasks of all the different groups that make up society, we want to point to the specific rights and duties of some of the persons and institutions whose work for justice will be particularly important to the future of the United States economy. These rights and duties are among the concrete implications of the principle of subsidiarity. Further implications will be discussed in Chapter IV of this letter.

1. Working People and Labor Unions

102. Though John Paul II's understanding of work is a very inclusive one, it fully applies to those customarily called "workers" or "labor" in the United States. Labor has great dignity, so great that all who are able to work are obligated to do so. The duty to work derives both from God's command and from a responsibility to one's own humanity and to the common good.[55] The virtue of industriousness is also an expression of a person's dignity and solidarity with others. All working people are called to contribute to the common good by seeking excellence in production and service.

103. Because work is this important, people have a right to employment. In return for their labor, workers have a right to wages and other benefits sufficient to sustain life in dignity. As Pope Leo XIII stated, every working person has "the right of securing things

---

[54] *Pastoral Constitution*, 31.
[55] *On Human Work*, 16.

to sustain life."[56] The way power is distributed in a free market economy frequently gives employers greater bargaining power than employees in the negotiation of labor contracts. Such unequal power may press workers into a choice between an inadequate wage and no wage at all. But justice, not charity, demands certain minimum guarantees. The provision of wages and other benefits sufficient to support a family in dignity is a basic necessity to prevent this exploitation of workers. The dignity of workers also requires adequate health care, security for old age or disability, unemployment compensation, healthful working conditions, weekly rest, periodic holidays for recreation and leisure, and reasonable security against arbitrary dismissal.[57] These provisions are all essential if workers are to be treated as persons rather than simply as a "factor of production."

104. The Church fully supports the right of workers to form unions or other associations to secure their rights to fair wages and working conditions. This is a specific application of the more general right to associate. In the words of Pope John Paul II, "The experience of history teaches that organizations of this type are an indispensable element of social life, especially in modern industrialized societies."[58] Unions may also legitimately resort to strikes where this is the only available means to the justice owed to workers.[59] No one may deny the right to organize without attacking human dignity itself. Therefore, we firmly oppose organized efforts, such as those regrettably now seen in this country, to break existing unions and prevent workers from organizing. Migrant agricultural workers today are particularly in need of the

---

[56] *Rerum Novarum*, 62; see also 9.
[57] *On Human Work*, 19.
[58] Ibid., 20.
[59] Ibid.

protection, including the right to organize and bargain collectively. U.S. labor law reform is needed to meet these problems as well as to provide more timely and effective remedies for unfair labor practices.

105. Denial of the right to organize has been pursued ruthlessly in many countries beyond our borders. We vehemently oppose violations of the freedom to associate, wherever they occur, for they are an intolerable attack on social solidarity.

106. Along with the rights of workers and unions go a number of important responsibilities. Individual workers have obligations to their employers, and trade unions also have duties to society as a whole. Union management in particular carries a strong responsibility for the good name of the entire union movement. Workers must use their collective power to contribute to the well-being of the whole community and should avoid pressing demands whose fulfillment would damage the common good and the rights of more vulnerable members of society.[60] It should be noted, however, that wages paid to workers are but one of the factors affecting the competitiveness of industries. Thus, it is unfair to expect unions to make concessions if managers and shareholders do not make at least equal sacrifices.

107. Many U.S. unions have exercised leadership in the struggle for justice for minorities and women. Racial and sexual discrimination, however, have blotted the record of some unions. Organized labor has a responsibility to work positively toward eliminating the injustice this discrimination has caused.

108. Perhaps the greatest challenge facing United States workers and unions today is that of developing a new vision of their role in the United States economy of the future. The labor movement in the United States stands at a crucial moment. The dynamism of the

---

[60] Ibid.

54

unions that led to their rapid growth in the middle decades of this century has been replaced by a decrease in the percentage of U.S. workers who are organized. American workers are under heavy pressures today that threaten their jobs. The restrictions on the right to organize in many countries abroad make labor costs lower there, threaten American workers and their jobs, and lead to the exploitation of workers in these countries. In these difficult circumstances, guaranteeing the rights of U.S. workers calls for imaginative vision and creative new steps, not reactive or simply defensive strategies. For example, organized labor can play a very important role in helping to provide the education and training needed to help keep workers employable. Unions can also help both their own members and workers in developing countries by increasing their international efforts. A vital labor movement will be one that looks to the future with a deepened sense of global interdependence.

109. There are many signs that these challenges are being discussed by creative labor leaders today. Deeper and broader discussions of this sort are needed. This does not mean that only organized labor faces these new problems. All other sectors and institutions in the U.S. economy need similar vision and imagination. Indeed new forms of cooperation among labor, management, government, and other social groups are essential, and will be discussed in Chapter IV of this letter.

2. Owners and Managers

110. The economy's success in fulfilling the demands of justice will depend on how its vast resources and wealth are managed. Property owners, managers, and investors of financial capital must all contribute to creating a more just society. Securing economic

justice depends heavily on the leadership of men and women in business and on wise investment by private enterprises. Pope John Paul II has pointed out, "The degree of well-being which society today enjoys would be unthinkable without the dynamic figure of the business person, whose function consists of organizing human labor and the means of production so as to give rise to the goods and services necessary for the prosperity and progress of the community."[61] The freedom of entrepreneurship, business, and finance should be protected, but the accountability of this freedom to the common good and the norms of justice must be assured.

111. Persons in management face many hard choices each day, choices on which the well-being of many others depends. Commitment to the public good and not simply the private good of their firms is at the heart of what it means to call their work a vocation and not simply a career or a job. We believe that the norms and priorities discussed in this letter can be of help as they pursue their important tasks. The duties of individuals in the business world, however, do not exhaust the ethical dimensions of business and finance. The size of a firm or bank is in many cases an indicator of relative power. Large corporations and large financial institutions have considerable power to help shape economic institutions within the United States and throughout the world. With this power goes responsibility and the need for those who manage it to be held to moral and institutional accountability.

112. Business and finance have the duty to be faithful trustees of the resources at their disposal. No one can ever own capital resources absolutely or control

---

[61] Pope John Paul II, Address to Business Men and Economic Managers (Milan, May 22, 1983) in *L'Osservatore Romano*, weekly edition in English (June 20, 1983): 9:1.

their use without regard for others and society as a whole.[62] This applies first of all to land and natural resources. Short-term profits reaped at the cost of depletion of natural resources or the pollution of the environment violate this trust.

113. Resources created by human industry are also held in trust. Owners and managers have not created this capital on their own. They have benefited from the work of many others and from the local communities that support their endeavors.[63] They are accountable to these workers and communities when making decisions. For example, reinvestment in technological innovation is often crucial for the long-term viability of a firm. The use of financial resources solely in pursuit of short-term profits can stunt the production of needed goods and services; a broader vision of managerial responsibility is needed.

114. The Catholic tradition has long defended the right to private ownership of productive property.[64] This right is an important element in a just economic policy. It enlarges our capacity for creativity and initiative.[65] Small and medium-sized farms, businesses, and entrepreneurial enterprises are among the most creative and efficient sectors of our economy. They should be highly valued by the people of the United States, as are land ownership and home ownership. Widespread distribution of property can help avoid excessive concentration of economic and political power. For these reasons ownership should be made possible for a broad sector of our population.[66]

---

[62] Thomas Aquinas, *Summa Theologiae*, IIa, IIae, q. 66.

[63] As Pope John Paul II has stated: "This gigantic and powerful instrument—the whole collection of the means of production that in a sense are considered synonymous with 'capital'—is the result of work and bears the signs of human labor" *On Human Work*, 12.

[64] *Rerum Novarum*, 10, 15, 36.

[65] *Mater et Magistra*, 109.

[66] *Rerum Novarum*, 65, 66; *Mater et Magistra*, 115.

115. The common good may sometimes demand that the right to own be limited by public involvement in the planning or ownership of certain sectors of the economy. Support of private ownership does not mean that anyone has the right to unlimited accumulation of wealth. "Private property does not constitute for anyone an absolute or unconditioned right. No one is justified in keeping for his exclusive use what he does not need, when others lack necessities."[67] Pope John Paul II has referred to limits placed on ownership by the duty to serve the common good as a "social mortgage" on private property.[68] For example, these limits are the basis of society's exercise of eminent domain over privately owned land needed for roads or other essential public goods. The Church's teaching opposes collectivist and statist economic approaches. But it also rejects the notion that a free market automatically produces justice. Therefore, as Pope John Paul II has argued, "One cannot exclude the socialization, in suitable conditions, of certain means of production."[69] The determination of when such conditions exist must be made on a case by case basis in light of the demands of the common good.

116. United States business and financial enterprises can also help determine the justice or injustice of the world economy. They are not all-powerful, but their real power is unquestionable. Transnational corporations and financial institutions can make positive contributions to development and global solidarity. Pope John Paul II has pointed out, however, that the desire to maximize profits and reduce the cost of natural resources and labor has often tempted these transnational enterprises to behavior that increases

---

[67] *On the Development of Peoples*, 23.
[68] Pope John Paul II, Opening Address at the Puebla Conference (Puebla, Mexico, January 28, 1979) in John Eagleson and Philip Scharper, eds., *Puebla and Beyond*, 67.
[69] *On Human Work*, 14.

inequality and decreases the stability of the international order.[70] By collaborating with those national governments that serve their citizens justly and with intergovernmental agencies, these corporations can contribute to overcoming the desperate plight of many persons throughout the world.

117. Business people, managers, investors, and financiers follow a vital Christian vocation when they act responsibly and seek the common good. We encourage and support a renewed sense of vocation in the business community. We also recognize that the way business people serve society is governed and limited by the incentives which flow from tax policies, the availability of credit, and other public policies.

118. Businesses have a right to an institutional framework that does not penalize enterprises that act responsibly. Governments must provide regulations and a system of taxation which encourage firms to preserve the environment, employ disadvantaged workers, and create jobs in depressed areas. Managers and stockholders should not be torn between their responsibilities to their organizations and their responsibilities toward society as a whole.

3. Citizens and Government

119. In addition to rights and duties related to specific roles in the economy, everyone has obligations based simply on membership in the social community. By fulfilling these duties, we create a true commonwealth. Volunteering time, talent, and money to work for greater justice is a fundamental expression of Christian love and social solidarity. All who have more than they need must come to the aid of the poor. People with professional or technical skills needed to enhance the lives of others have a duty to share them.

---

[70] Ibid., 17.

And the poor have similar obligations: to work together as individuals and families to build up their communities by acts of social solidarity and justice. These voluntary efforts to overcome injustice are part of the Christian vocation.

120. Every citizen also has the responsibility to work to secure justice and human rights through an organized social response. In the words of Pius XI, "Charity will never be true charity unless it takes justice into account. . . . Let no one attempt with small gifts of charity to exempt himself from the great duties imposed by justice."[71] The guaranteeing of basic justice for all is not an optional expression of largesse but an inescapable duty for the whole of society.

121. The traditional distinction between society and the state in Catholic social teaching provides the basic framework for such organized public efforts. The Church opposes all statist and totalitarian approaches to socioeconomic questions. Social life is richer than governmental power can encompass. All groups that compose society have responsibilities to respond to the demands of justice. We have just outlined some of the duties of labor unions and business and financial enterprises. These must be supplemented by initiatives by local community groups, professional associations, educational institutions, churches, and synagogues. All the groups that give life to this society have important roles to play in the pursuit of economic justice.

122. For this reason, it is all the more significant that the teachings of the Church insist that *government has a moral function: protecting human rights and securing basic justice for all members of the commonwealth.*[72] Society as a whole and in all its diversity is responsible for building up the common good. But it is government's

---

[71] *Divini Redemptoris,* 49.
[72] *Peace on Earth,* 60-62.

role to guarantee the minimum conditions that make this rich social activity possible, namely, human rights and justice.[73] This obligation also falls on individual citizens as they choose their representatives and participate in shaping public opinion.

123. More specifically, it is the responsibility of all citizens, acting through their government, to assist and empower the poor, the disadvantaged, the handicapped, and the unemployed. Government should assume a positive role in generating employment and establishing fair labor practices, in guaranteeing the provision and maintenance of the economy's infrastructure, such as roads, bridges, harbors, public means of communication, and transport. It should regulate trade and commerce in the interest of fairness.[74] Government may levy the taxes necessary to meet these responsibilities, and citizens have a moral obligation to pay those taxes. The way society responds to the needs of the poor through its public

---

[73] Vatican Council II, *Declaration on Religious Freedom* (*Dignitatis Humanae*), 6. See John Courtney Murray, *The Problem of Religious Freedom*, Woodstock Papers, no. 7 (Westminster, Md.: Newman Press, 1965).

[74] *Peace on Earth*, 63-64. *Quadragesimo Anno*, 80. In *Rerum Novarum* Pope Leo XIII set down the basic norm that determines when government intervention is called for: "If, therefore, any injury has been done to or threatens either the common good or the interests of individual groups, which injury cannot in any other way be repaired or prevented, it is necessary for public authority to intervene" *Rerum Novarum*, 52. Pope John XXIII synthesized the Church's understanding of the function of governmental intervention this way: "The State, whose purpose is the realization of the common good in the temporal order, can by no means disregard the economic activity of its citizens. Indeed it should be present to promote in suitable manner the production of a sufficient supply of material goods, . . . contribute actively to the betterment of the living conditions of workers, . . . see to it that labor agreements are entered into according to the norms of justice and equity, and that in the environment of work the dignity of the human being is not violated either in body or spirit" *Mater et Magistra*, 20-21.

61

policies is the litmus test of its justice or injustice. The political debate about these policies is the indispensable forum for dealing with the conflicts and trade-offs that will always be present in the pursuit of a more just economy.

124. The primary norm for determining the scope and limits of governmental intervention is the "principle of subsidiarity" cited above. This principle states that, in order to protect basic justice, government should undertake only those initiatives which exceed the capacity of individuals or private groups acting independently. Government should not replace or destroy smaller communities and individual initiative. Rather it should help them to contribute more effectively to social well-being and supplement their activity when the demands of justice exceed their capacities. This does not mean, however, that the government that governs least governs best. Rather it defines good government intervention as that which truly "helps" other social groups contribute to the common good by directing, urging, restraining, and regulating economic activity as "the occasion requires and necessity demands."[75] This calls for cooperation and consensus-building among the diverse agents in our economic life, including government. The precise form of government involvement in this process cannot be determined in the abstract. It will depend on an assessment of specific needs and the most effective ways to address them.

D. Christian Hope and the Courage To Act

125. The Christian vision is based on the conviction that God has destined the human race and all creation

---

[75] *Quadragesimo Anno*, 79.

for "a kingdom of truth and life, of holiness and grace, of justice, love, and peace."[76] This conviction gives Christians strong hope as they face the economic struggles of the world today. This hope is not a naive optimism that imagines that simple formulas for creating a fully just society are ready at hand. The Church's experience through history and in nations throughout the world today has made it wary of all ideologies that claim to have the final answer to humanity's problems.[77] Christian hope has a much stronger foundation than such ideologies, for it rests on the knowledge that God is at work in the world, "preparing a new dwelling place and a new earth where justice will abide."[78]

126. This hope stimulates and strengthens Christian efforts to create a more just economic order in spite of difficulties and setbacks.[79] Christian hope is strong and resilient, for it is rooted in a faith that knows that the fullness of life comes to those who follow Christ in the way of the Cross. In pursuit of concrete solutions, all members of the Christian community are called to an ever finer discernment of the hurts and opportunities in the world around them, in order to respond to the most pressing needs and thus build up a more just society.[80] This is a communal task calling for dialogue, experimentation, and imagination. It also calls for deep faith and courageous love.

---

[76] Preface for the Feast of Christ the King, *The Sacramentary of the Roman Missal.*
[77] *Octogesima Adveniens,* 26-35.
[78] *Pastoral Constitution,* 39.
[79] Ibid.
[80] *Octogesima Adveniens,* 42.

Chapter III

SELECTED
ECONOMIC POLICY ISSUES

127. We have outlined this moral vision as a guide to all who seek to be faithful to the Gospel in their daily economic decisions and as a challenge to transform the economic arrangements that shape our lives and our world. These arrangements embody and communicate social values and therefore have moral significance both in themselves and in their effects. Christians, like all people, must be concerned about how the concrete outcomes of their economic activity serve human dignity; they must assess the extent to which the structures and practices of the economy support or undermine their moral vision.

128. Such an assessment of economic practices, structures, and outcomes leads to a variety of conclusions. Some people argue that an unfettered free-market economy, where owners, workers, and consumers pursue their enlightened self-interest, provides the greatest possible liberty, material welfare, and equity. The policy implication of this view is to intervene in the economy as little as possible because it is such a delicate mechanism that any attempt to improve it is likely to have the opposite effect. Others argue that the capitalist system is inherently inequitable and therefore contradictory to the demands of Christian morality, for it is based on acquisitiveness, competi-

tion, and self-centered individualism. They assert that capitalism is fatally flawed and must be replaced by a radically different system that abolishes private property, the profit motive, and the free market.

129. Catholic social teaching has traditionally rejected these ideological extremes because they are likely to produce results contrary to human dignity and economic justice.[1] Starting with the assumption that the economy has been created by human beings and can be changed by them, the Church works for improvement in a variety of economic and political contexts; but it is not the Church's role to create or promote a specific new economic system. Rather, the Church must encourage all reforms that hold out hope of transforming our economic arrangements into a fuller systemic realization of the Christian moral vision. The Church must also stand ready to challenge practices and institutions that impede or carry us farther away from realizing this vision.

130. In short, the Church is not bound to any particular economic, political, or social system; it has lived with many forms of economic and social organization and will continue to do so, evaluating each according to moral and ethical principles: What is the impact of the system on people? Does it support or threaten human dignity?

131. In this document we offer reflections on the particular reality that is the U.S. economy. In doing so we are aware of the need to address not only individual issues within the economy but also the larger question of the economic system itself. Our approach in analyzing the U.S. economy is pragmatic and evolutionary in nature. We live in a "mixed" economic system which is the product of a long history of reform and adjustment. It is in the spirit of this American pragmatic tradition of reform that we seek to continue

---

[1] *Octogesima Adveniens*, 26-41; and *On Human Work*, 7, 13.

the search for a more just economy. Our nation has many assets to employ in this quest—vast economic, technological, and human resources and a system of representative government through which we can all help shape economic decisions.

132. Although we have chosen in this chapter to focus primarily on some aspects of the economy where we think reforms are realistically possible, we also emphasize that Catholic social teaching bears directly on larger questions concerning the economic system itself and the values it expresses—questions that cannot be ignored in the Catholic vision of economic justice.[2] For example, does our economic system place more emphasis on maximizing profits than on meeting human needs and fostering human dignity? Does our economy distribute its benefits equitably or does it concentrate power and resources in the hands of a few? Does it promote excessive materialism and individualism? Does is adequately protect the environment and the nation's natural resources? Does it direct too many scarce resources to military purposes? These and other basic questions about the economy need to be scrutinized in light of the ethical norms we have outlined. We urge continuing exploration of these systemic questions in a more comprehensive way than this document permits.

133. We have selected the following subjects to address here: 1) employment, 2) poverty, 3) food and agriculture, and 4) the U.S. role in the global economy. These topics were chosen because of their relevance to both the economic "signs of the times" and the ethical norms of our tradition. Each exemplifies U.S. policies that are basic to the establishment of economic justice in the nation and the world, and each illustrates key moral principles and norms for action from Catholic social teaching. Our treatment of these issues does

---

[2] *Program of Social Reconstruction*, 33-40.

67

not constitute a comprehensive analysis of the U.S. economy. We emphasize that these are illustrative topics intended to exemplify the interaction of moral values and economic issues in our day, not to encompass all such values and issues. This document is not a technical blueprint for economic reform. Rather, it is an attempt to foster a serious moral analysis leading to a more just economy.

134. In focusing on some of the central economic issues and choices in American life in the light of moral principles, we are aware that the movement from principle to policy is complex and difficult and that although moral values are essential in determining public policies, they do not dictate specific solutions. They must interact with empirical data, with historical, social, and political realities, and with competing demands on limited resources. The soundness of our prudential judgments depends not only on the moral force of our principles, but also on the accuracy of our information and the validity of our assumptions.

135. Our judgments and recommendations on specific economic issues, therefore, do not carry the same moral authority as our statements of universal moral principles and formal church teaching; the former are related to circumstances which can change or which can be interpreted differently by people of good will. We expect and welcome debate on our specific policy recommendations. Nevertheless, we want our statements on these matters to be given serious consideration by Catholics as they determine whether their own moral judgments are consistent with the Gospel and with Catholic social teaching. We believe that differences on complex economic questions should be expressed in a spirit of mutual respect and open dialogue.[3]

------

[3] See *The Challenge of Peace: God's Promise and Our Response*, 9-10.

A. Employment

136. Full employment is the foundation of a just economy. The most urgent priority for domestic economic policy is the creation of new jobs with adequate pay and decent working conditions. We must make it possible as a nation for every one who is seeking a job to find employment within a reasonable amount of time. Our emphasis on this goal is based on the conviction that human work has a special dignity and is a key to achieving justice in society.[4]

137. Employment is a basic right, a right which protects the freedom of all to participate in the economic life of society. It is a right which flows from the principles of justice which we have outlined above. Corresponding to this right is the duty on the part of society to ensure that the right is protected. The importance of this right is evident in the fact that for most people employment is crucial to self-realization and essential to the fulfillment of material needs. Since so few in our economy own productive property, employment also forms the first line of defense against poverty. Jobs benefit society as well as workers, for they enable more people to contribute to the common good and to the productivity required for a healthy economy.

1. The Scope and Effects of Unemployment

138. Joblessness is becoming a more widespread and deep-seated problem in our nation. There are about 8 million people in the United States looking for a job who cannot find one. They represent about

---

[4] *On Human Work*, 3.

7 percent of the labor force.[5] The official rate of unemployment does not include those who have given up looking for work or those who are working part-time, but want to work full-time. When these categories are added, it becomes clear that about one-eighth of the workforce is directly affected by unemployment.[6] The severity of the unemployment problem is compounded by the fact that almost three-fourths of those who are unemployed receive no unemployment insurance benefits.[7]

139. In recent years there has been a steady trend toward higher and higher levels of unemployment, even in good times. Between 1950 and 1980 the annual unemployment rate exceeded current levels only during the recession years of 1975 and 1976. Periods of economic recovery during these three decades brought unemployment rates down to 3 and 4 percent. Since 1979, however, the rate has generally been above 7 percent.

140. Who are the unemployed? Blacks, Hispanics, Native Americans, young adults, female heads of households, and those who are inadequately educated are represented disproportionately among the ranks of the unemployed. The unemployment rate among minorities is almost twice as high as the rate among whites. For female heads of households the unemployment rate is over 10 percent. Among black

---

[5] U.S. Department of Labor, Bureau of Labor Statistics, *The Employment Situation: April 1986* (May 1986).

[6] Full Employment Action Council, *Employment in America: Illusory Recovery in a Decade of Decline* (Washington, D.C., February 1985), 19. Calculations based on data from the U.S. Department of Labor's Bureau of Labor Statistics.

[7] U.S. Department of Labor, Bureau of Labor Statistics, *The Employment Situation: August 1985*; and U. S. Department of Labor, Employment and Training Administration, *Unemployment Insurance Claims*, Reference week of June 22, 1985.

teenagers, unemployment reaches the scandalous rate of more than one in three.[8]

141. The severe human costs of high unemployment levels become vividly clear when we examine the impact of joblessness on human lives and human dignity. It is a deep conviction of American culture that work is central to the freedom and well-being of people. The unemployed often come to feel they are worthless and without a productive role in society. Each day they are unemployed our society tells them: We don't need your talent. We don't need your initiative. We don't need *you*. Unemployment takes a terrible toll on the health and stability of both individuals and families. It gives rise to family quarrels, greater consumption of alcohol, child abuse, spouse abuse, divorce, and higher rates of infant mortality.[9] People who are unemployed often feel that society blames them for being unemployed. Very few people survive long periods of unemployment without some psychological damage even if they have sufficient funds to meet their needs.[10] At the extreme, the strains

---

[8] *The Employment Situation: August 1985.*

[9] Brenner, "Fetal, Infant and Maternal Mortality during Periods of Economic Instability," *International Journal of Health Services* (Summer 1973); P. H. Ellison, "Neurology of Hard Times," *Clinical Pediatrics* (March 1977); S. V. Kasl and S. Cobb, "Some Mental Health Consequences of Plant Closings and Job Loss," in L. Ferman and J. P. Gordus, eds., *Mental Health and the Economy* (Kalamazoo, Mich.: W. E. Upjohn Institute for Employment Research, 1979), 255-300; L. E. Kopolow and F. M. Ochberg, "Spinoff from a Downward Swing," *Mental Health* 59 (Summer 1975); D. Shaw, "Unemployment Hurts More than the Pocketbook," *Today's Health* (March 1978).

[10] Richard M. Cohn, *The Consequences of Unemployment on Evaluation of Self,* Doctoral dissertation, Department of Psychology (University of Michigan, 1977); John A. Garraty, *Unemployment in History: Economic Thought and Public Policy* (New York: Harper and Row, 1978); Harry Maurer, *Not Working: An Oral History of the Unemployed* (New York: Holt, Rinehart, and Winston, 1979).

of job loss may drive individuals to suicide.[11]

142. In addition to the terrible waste of individual talent and creativity, unemployment also harms society at large. Jobless people pay little or no taxes, thus lowering the revenues for cities, states, and the federal government. At the same time, rising unemployment requires greater expenditures for unemployment compensation, food stamps, welfare, and other assistance. It is estimated that in 1986, for every one percentage point increase in the rate of unemployment, there will be roughly a $40 billion increase in the federal deficit.[12] The costs to society are also evident in the rise in crime associated with joblessness. The Federal Bureau of Prisons reports that increases in unemployment have been followed by increases in the prison population. Other studies have shown links between the rate of joblessness and the frequency of homicides, robberies, larcenies, narcotics arrests, and youth crimes.[13]

143. Our own experiences with the individuals, families, and communities that suffer the burdens of unemployment compel us to the conviction that as a nation we simply cannot afford to have millions of able-bodied men and women unemployed. We cannot afford the economic costs, the social dislocation, and the enormous human tragedies caused by unemployment. In the end, however, what we can least afford

---

[11] M. Harvey Brenner, *Estimating the Social Cost of National Economic Policy* (U.S. Congress, Joint Economic Committee, 1976); see Brenner, *Mental Illness and the Economy* (Cambridge, Mass.: Harvard University Press, 1973).

[12] Congressional Budget Office, *Economic and Budget Outlook: FY 1986—FY 1990* (Washington, D.C., February 1985), 75.

[13] *Correlation of Unemployment and Federal Prison Population* (Washington, D.C.: U.S. Bureau of Prisons, March 1975); M. Yeager, "Unemployment and Imprisonment," *Journal of Criminal Law and Criminology* 70:4 (1979); Testimony of M. H. Brenner in *Unemployment and Crime* (U.S. Congress, House Hearings, 1977,) 25.

is the assault on human dignity that occurs when millions are left without adequate employment. Therefore, we cannot but conclude that current levels of unemployment are intolerable, and they impose on us a moral obligation to work for policies that will reduce joblessness.

2. Unemployment in a Changing Economy

144. The structure of the U.S. economy is undergoing a transformation that affects both the quantity and the quality of jobs in our nation. The size and makeup of the workforce, for example, have changed markedly in recent years. For a number of reasons, there are now more people in the labor market than ever before in our history. Population growth has pushed up the supply of potential workers. In addition, large numbers of women have entered the labor force not only in order to put their talents and education to greater use, but also out of economic necessity. Many families need two salaries if they are to live in a decently human fashion. Female-headed households often depend heavily on the mother's income to stay off the welfare rolls. Immigrants seeking a better existence in the United States have also added to the size of the labor force. These demographic changes, however, cannot fully explain the higher levels of unemployment.

145. Technological changes are also having dramatic impacts on the employment picture in the United States. Advancing technology brings many benefits, but it can also bring social and economic costs, including the downgrading and displacement of workers. High technology and advanced automation are changing the very face of our nation's industries and occupations. In the 1970s, about 90 percent of all new jobs were in service occupations. By 1990, service industries are expected to employ 72 percent of the labor

73

force. Much of the job growth in the 1980s is expected to be in traditionally low-paying, high-turnover jobs such as sales, clerical, janitorial, and food service.[14] Too often these jobs do not have career ladders leading to higher skilled, higher paying jobs. Thus, the changing industrial and occupational mix in the U.S. economy could result in a shift toward lower paying and lower skilled jobs.

146. Increased competition in world markets is another factor influencing the rate of joblessness in our nation. Many other exporting nations have acquired and developed up-to-the-minute technology, enabling them to increase productivity dramatically. Combined with very low wages in many nations, this has allowed them to gain a larger share of the U.S. market to cut into U.S. export markets. At the same time many corporations have closed plants in the United States and moved their capital, technology, and jobs to foreign affiliates.

147. Discrimination in employment is one of the causes for high rates of joblessness and low pay among racial minorities and women. Beyond the normal problems of locating a job, blacks, Hispanics, Native Americans, immigrants, and other minorities bear this added burden of discrimination. Discrimination against women is compounded by the lack of adequate child care services and by the unwillingness of many employers to provide flexible employment or extend fringe benefits to part-time employees.

148. High levels of defense spending also have an effect on the number of jobs in our economy. In our pastoral letter, *The Challenge of Peace*, we noted the serious economic distortions caused by the arms race and the disastrous effects that it has on society's ability to care for the poor and the needy. Employment is

---

[14] Committee on the Evolution of Work, AFL-CIO, *The Future of Work* (Washington, D.C.: AFL-CIO, 1983), 11.

one area in which this interconnection is very evident. The hundreds of billions of dollars spent by our nation each year on the arms race create a massive drain on the U.S. economy as well as a very serious "brain drain." Such spending on the arms race means a net loss in the number of jobs created in the economy, because defense industries are less labor-intensive than other major sectors of the economy.[15] Moreover, nearly half of the American scientific and engineering force works in defense-related programs and over 60 percent of the entire federal research and development budget goes to the military.[16] We must ask whether our nation will ever be able to modernize our economy and achieve full employment if we continue to devote so much of our financial and human resources to defense-related activities.

149. These are some of the factors that have driven up the rate of unemployment in recent years. Although our economy has created more than 20 million new jobs since 1970,[17] there continues to be a chronic and growing job shortage. In the face of this challenge,

[15] Congressional Budget Office, *Defense Spending and the Economy* (Washington, D.C.: Government Printing Office, 1983). See also Michael Edelstein, *The Economic Impact of Military Spending* (New York: Council on Economic Priorities, 1977); and Robert De Grasse, Jr., *Military Expansion, Economic Decline* (New York: Council on Economic Priorities, 1983). See also U.S. Department of Labor, Bureau of Labor Statistics Report, "Structure of the U.S. Economy in 1980 and 1985" (Washington, D.C.: Government Printing Office, 1975); and Marion Anderson, *The Empty Pork Barrel* (Lansing, Mich.: Employment Research Associates, 1982).

[16] U.S. Office of Management and Budget, *Historical Tables*, Budget of the United States Government Fiscal Year 1986 (Washington, D.C.: U.S. Government Printing Office, 1985). Table 10.2, 10.2(3). See also, National Science Foundation Report, "Characteristics of Experienced Scientists and Engineers" (1978), Detailed Statistical Tables (Washington, D.C.: U.S. Government Printing Office, 1978).

[17] "Statistical Supplement to International Comparison of Unemployment," Bureau of Labor Statistics, (May 1984): 7. Unpublished.

our nation's economic institutions have failed to adapt adequately and rapidly enough. For example, failure to invest sufficiently in certain industries and regions, inadequate education and training for new workers, and insufficient mechanisms to assist workers displaced by new technology have added to the unemployment problem.

150. Generating an adequate number of jobs in our economy is a complex task in view of the changing and diverse nature of the problem. It involves numerous trade-offs and substantial costs. Nevertheless, it is not an impossible task. Achieving the goal of full employment may require major adjustments and creative strategies that go beyond the limits of existing policies and institutions, but it is a task we must undertake.

3. Guidelines for Action

151. We recommend that the nation make a major new commitment to achieve full employment. At present there is nominal endorsement of the full employment ideal, but no firm commitment to bringing it about. If every effort were now being made to create the jobs required, one might argue that the situation today is the best we can do. But such is not the case. The country is doing far less than it might to generate employment.

152. Over the last decade, economists, policy makers, and the general public have shown greater willingness to tolerate unemployment levels of 6 to 7 percent or even more.[18] Although we recognize the

---

[18] Isabel V. Sawhill and Charles F. Stone state the prevailing view among economists this way: "High employment is usually defined as the rate of unemployment consistent with no additional inflation, a rate currently believed by many, but not all, economists to be in the neighborhood of 6 percent." "The Economy: The Key

complexities and trade-offs involved in reducing unemployment, we believe that 6 to 7 percent unemployment is neither inevitable nor acceptable. While a zero unemployment rate is clearly impossible in an economy where people are constantly entering the job market and others are changing jobs, appropriate policies and concerted private and public action can improve the situation considerably, if we have the will to do so. No economy can be considered truly healthy when so many millions of people are denied jobs by forces outside their control. The acceptance of present unemployment rates would have been unthinkable twenty years ago. It should be regarded as intolerable today.

153. We must first establish a consensus that everyone has a right to employment. Then the burden of securing full employment falls on all of us—policy makers, business, labor, and the general public—to create and implement the mechanisms to protect that right. We must work for the formation of a new national consensus and mobilize the necessary political will at all levels to make the goal of full employment a reality.

154. Expanding employment in our nation will require significant steps in both the private and public sectors, as well as joint action between them. Private initiative and entrepreneurship are essential to this task, for the private sector accounts for about 80 percent of the jobs in the United States, and most new jobs are being created there.[19] Thus, a viable strategy for employment generation must assume that a large

---

to Success," in John L. Palmer and Isabel V. Sawhill, eds., *The Reagan Record: An Assessment of America's Changing Domestic Priorities* (Cambridge, Mass.: Bollinger, 1984), 72. See also Stanley Fischer and Rudiger Dornbusch, *Economics* (New York: McGraw-Hill, 1983), 731-743.

[19] W. L. Birch, "Who Creates Jobs?," *The Public Interest* 65 (Fall 1981): 3-14.

part of the solution will be with private firms and small businesses. At the same time, it must be recognized that government has a prominent and indispensable role to play in addressing the problem of unemployment. The market alone will not automatically produce full employment. Therefore, the government must act to ensure that this goal is achieved by coordinating general economic policies, by job creation programs, and by other appropriate policy measures.

155. Effective action against unemployment will require a careful mix of general economic policies and targeted employment programs. Taken together, these policies and programs should have full employment as their number one goal.

a. General Economic Policies

156. The general or macroeconomic policies of the federal government are essential tools for encouraging the steady economic growth that produces more and better jobs in the economy. *We recommend that the fiscal and monetary policies of the nation—such as federal spending, tax, and interest rate policies—should be coordinated so as to achieve the goal of full employment.*

157. General economic policies that attempt to expand employment must also deal with the problem of inflation.[20] The risk of inflationary pressures re-

[20] Martin Neil Baily and Arthur M. Okun, eds., *The Battle Against Unemployment and Inflation*, third edition (New York: Norton, 1982); and Martin Neil Baily, "Labor Market Performance, Competition and Inflation," in Baily, ed., *Workers, Jobs and Inflation* (Washington, D.C.: The Brookings Institution, 1982). See also, Lawrence Klein, "Reducing Unemployment Without Inflation"; and James Tobin, "Unemployment, Poverty, and Economic Policy," testimony before the Subcommittee on Economic Stabilization, U.S. House of Representatives Committee on Banking, Finance and Urban Affairs (March 19, 1985), serial no. 99-5 (Washington, D.C.: U.S. Government Printing Office, 1985), 15-18, 31-33.

sulting from such expansionary policies is very real. Our response to this risk, however, must not be to abandon the goal of full employment, but to develop effective policies that keep inflation under control.

158. While economic growth is an important and necessary condition for the reduction of unemployment, it is not sufficient in and of itself. In order to work for full employment and restrain inflation, it is also necessary to adopt more specific programs and policies targeted toward particular aspects of the unemployment problem.[21]

b. Targeted Employment Programs

159. (1) *We recommend expansion of job-training and apprenticeship programs in the private sector administered and supported jointly by business, labor unions, and government.* Any comprehensive employment strategy must include systematic means of developing the technical and professional skills needed for a dynamic and productive economy. Investment in a skilled work force is a prerequisite both for sustaining economic growth and achieving greater justice in the United States. The obligation to contribute to this investment falls on both the private and public sectors. Today business, labor, and government need to coordinate their efforts and pool their resources to promote a substantial increase in the number of apprenticeship programs and to expand on-the-job training programs. We recommend a national commitment to eradicate illiteracy and to provide people with the skills necessary to adapt to the changing demands of employment.

160. With the rapid pace of technological change,

---

[21] Tobin, "Unemployment, Poverty, and Economic Policy"; and Klein, "Reducing Unemployment Without Inflation."

continuing education and training are even more important today than in the past. Businesses have a stake in providing it, for skilled workers are essential to increased productivity. Labor unions should support it, for their members are increasingly vulnerable to displacement and job loss unless they continue to develop their skills and their flexibility on the job. Local communities have a stake as well, for their economic well-being will suffer serious harm if local industries fail to develop and are forced to shut down.

161. The best medicine for the disease of plant-closings is prevention. Prevention depends not only on sustained capital investment to enhance productivity through advanced technology but also on the training and retraining of workers within the private sector. In circumstances where plants are forced to shut down, management, labor unions, and local communities must see to it that workers are not simply cast aside. Retraining programs will be even more urgently needed in these circumstances.

162. (2) *We recommend increased support for direct job creation programs targeted on the long-term unemployed and those with special needs.* Such programs can take the form of direct public service employment and also of public subsidies for employment in the private sector. Both approaches would provide jobs for those with low skills less expensively and with less inflation than would general stimulation of the economy.[22] The cost of providing jobs must also be balanced against the savings realized by the government through decreased welfare and unemployment insurance expenditures and increased revenues from the taxes paid by the newly employed.

163. Government funds, if used effectively, can also stimulate private sector jobs for the long-term un-

---

[22] Robert H. Haveman, "Toward Efficiency and Equity through Direct Job Creation," *Social Policy* 11:1 (May/June 1980): 48.

employed and for groups particularly hard to employ. Experiments need to be conducted on the precise ways such subsidies would most successfully attract business participation and ensure the generation of permanent jobs.

164. These job generation efforts should aim specifically at bringing marginalized persons into the labor force. They should produce a net increase in the number of jobs rather than displacing the burden of unemployment from one group of persons to another. They should also be aimed at long-term jobs and should include the necessary supportive services to assist the unemployed in finding and keeping jobs.

165. Jobs that are created should produce goods and services needed and valued by society. It is both good common sense and sound economics to create jobs directly for the purpose of meeting society's unmet needs. Across the nation, in every state and locality, there is ample evidence of social needs that are going unmet. Many of our parks and recreation facilities are in need of maintenance and repair. Many of the nation's bridges and highways are in disrepair. We have a desperate need for more low-income housing. Our educational systems, day-care services, senior citizen services, and other community programs need to be expanded. These and many other elements of our national life are areas of unmet need. At the same time, there are more than 8 million Americans looking for productive and useful work. Surely we have the capacity to match these needs by giving Americans who are anxious to work a chance for productive employment in jobs that are waiting to be done. The overriding moral value of enabling jobless persons to achieve a new sense of dignity and personal worth through employment also strongly recommends these programs.

166. These job creation efforts will require increased collaboration and fresh alliances between the

private and public sectors at all levels. There are already a number of examples of how such efforts can be successful.[23] We believe that the potential of these kinds of partnerships has only begun to be tapped.

c. Examining New Strategies

167. In addition to the actions suggested above, we believe there is also a need for careful examination and experimentation with alternative approaches that might improve both the quantity and quality of jobs. More extensive use of job sharing, flex time, and a reduced work week are among the topics that should continue to be on the agenda of public discussion. Consideration should also be given to the possibility of limiting or abolishing compulsory overtime work. Similarly, methods might be examined to discourage the overuse of part-time workers, who do not receive fringe benefits.[24] New strategies also need to be explored in the area of education and training for the hard-to-employ, displaced workers, the handicapped, and others with special needs. Particular attention is needed to achieve pay equity between men and

---

[23] William H. McCarthy, *Reducing Urban Unemployment: What Works at the Local Level* (Washington, D.C.: National League of Cities, October 1985); William Schweke, "States that Take the Lead on a New Industrial Policy," in Betty G. Lall, ed., *Economic Dislocation and Job Loss* (New York: Cornell University, New York State School of Industrial and Labor Relations, 1985), 97-106; David Robinson, *Training and Jobs Programs in Action: Case Studies in Private Sector Initiatives for the Hard to Employ* (New York: Committee for Economic Development, 1978). See also ch. IV of this pastoral letter.

[24] Rudy Oswald, "The Economy and Workers' Jobs, The Living Wage and a Voice," in John W. Houch and Oliver F. Williams, eds., *Catholic Social Teaching and the U.S. Economy: Working Papers for a Bishops' Pastoral* (Washington, D.C.: University Press of America, 1984), 77-89. On the subject of shortening the work week, Oswald points out that in the first 40 years of this century, the average work week fell from 60 hours to 40 hours. However, the standard work week has been unchanged now for almost 50 years.

women, as well as upgrading the pay scale and working conditions of traditionally low-paying jobs. The nation should renew its efforts to develop effective affirmative action policies that assist those who have been excluded by racial or sexual discrimination in the past. New strategies for improving job placement services at the national and local levels are also needed. Improving occupational safety is another important concern that deserves increased attention.

168. Much greater attention also needs to be devoted to the long-term task of converting some of the nation's military production to more peaceful and socially productive purposes. The nation needs to seek more effective ways to retool industries, to retrain workers, and to provide the necessary adjustment assistance for communities affected by this kind of economic conversion.

169. These are among the avenues that need to be explored in the search for just employment policies. A belief in the inherent dignity of human work and in the right to employment should motivate people in all sectors of society to carry on that search in new and creative ways.

B. Poverty

170. More than 33 million Americans—about one in every seven people in our nation—are poor by the government's official definition. The norms of human dignity and the preferential option for the poor compel us to confront this issue with a sense of urgency. Dealing with poverty is not a luxury to which our nation can attend when it finds the time and resources. Rather, it is a moral imperative of the highest priority.

171. Of particular concern is the fact that poverty has increased dramatically during the last decade. Since 1973 the poverty rate has increased by nearly a third. Although the recent recovery has brought a slight decline in the rate, it remains at a level that is higher than at almost any other time during the last two decades.[25]

172. As pastors we have seen firsthand the faces of poverty in our midst. Homeless people roam city streets in tattered clothing and sleep in doorways or on subway grates at night. Many of these are former mental patients released from state hospitals. Thousands stand in line at soup kitchens because they have no other way of feeding themselves. Millions of children are so poorly nourished that their physical and mental development are seriously harmed.[26] We have also seen the growing economic hardship and insecurity experienced by moderate-income Americans when they lose their jobs and their income due to forces beyond their control. These are alarming signs and trends. They pose for our nation an urgent moral and human challenge: to fashion a society where no one goes without the basic material necessities required for human dignity and growth.

173. Poverty can be described and defined in many different ways. It can include spiritual as well as material poverty. Likewise, its meaning changes depending on the historical, social, and economic setting. Poverty in our time is different from the more severe deprivation experienced in earlier centuries in the U.S. or in Third World nations today. Our discussion of poverty in this chapter is set within the context of

---

[25] U.S. Bureau of the Census, Current Population Reports, Series P-60, no. 149, *Money Income and Poverty Status of Families in the United States: 1984* (Washington, D.C.: U.S. Government Printing Office, 1985).
[26] Massachusetts Department of Public Health, *Massachusetts Nutrition Survey* (Boston, Mass.: 1983).

present-day American society. By poverty, we are referring here to the lack of sufficient material resources required for a decent life. We use the government's official definition of poverty, although we recognize its limits.[27]

1. Characteristics of Poverty

174. Poverty is not an isolated problem existing solely among a small number of anonymous people in our central cities. Nor is it limited to a dependent underclass or to specific groups in the United States. It is a condition experienced at some time by many people in different walks of life and in different circumstances. Many poor people are working but at

---

[27] There is considerable debate about the most suitable definition of poverty. Some argue that the government's official definition understates the number of the poor, and that a more adequate definition would indicate that as many as 50 million Americans are poor. For example, they note that the poverty line has declined sharply as a percent of median family income—from 48% in 1959 to 35% in 1983. Others argue that the official indicators should be reduced by the amount of in-kind benefits received by the poor, such as food stamps. By some calculations that would reduce the number counted as poor to about 12 million. We conclude that for present purposes the official government definition provides a suitable middle ground. That definition is based on a calculation that multiplies the cost of USDA's lowest cost food plan times three. The definition is adjusted for inflation each year.

Among other reasons for using the official definition is that it allows one to compare poverty figures over time. For additional readings on this topic see: L. Rainwater, *What Money Buys: Inequality and the Social Meanings of Income* (New York: Basic Books, 1975); id., *Persistent and Transitory Poverty: A New Look* (Cambridge, Mass.: Joint Center for Urban Studies, 1980); M. Orshansky, "How Poverty is Measured," *Monthly Labor Review* 92 (1969): 37-41; M. Anderson, *Welfare* (Stanford, Calif.: Hoover Institution Press, 1978); and Michael Harrington, *The New American Poverty* (New York: Holt, Rinehart, and Winston, 1984), 81-82.

wages insufficient to lift them out of poverty.[28] Others are unable to work and therefore dependent on outside sources of support. Still others are on the edge of poverty; although not officially defined as poor, they are economically insecure and at risk of falling into poverty.

175. While many of the poor manage to escape from beneath the official poverty line, others remain poor for extended periods of time. Long-term poverty is concentrated among racial minorities and families headed by women. It is also more likely to be found in rural areas and in the South.[29] Of the long-term poor, most are either working at wages too low to bring them above the poverty line or are retired, disabled, or parents of preschool children. Generally they are not in a position to work more hours than they do now.[30]

---

[28] Of those in poverty, 3 million work year-round and are still poor. Of the 22.2 million poor who are 15 years or over, more than 9 million work sometime during the year. Since 1979, the largest increases of poverty in absolute terms have been among those who work and are still poor. U.S. Bureau of the Census, *Money, Income and Poverty.*

[29] U.S. Bureau of the Census, Current Population Reports, series P-60, no. 149, 19. Blacks make up about 12% of the entire population but 62% of the long-term poor. Only 19% of the overall population live in families headed by women, but they make up 61% of the long-term poor. Twenty-eight percent of the nation's total population reside in nonmetropolitan areas, but 34% of the nation's poor live in these areas.

[30] G. J. Duncan et al., *Years of Poverty, Years of Plenty: The Changing Economic Fortunes of American Workers and Their Families* (Ann Arbor, Mich.: Institute for Social Research, The University of Michigan, 1984). This book is based on the Panel Study of Income Dynamics, a survey of 5,000 American families conducted annually by the Survey Research Center of the University of Michigan. See G. J. Duncan and J. N. Morgan, *Five Thousand American Families—Patterns of Economic Progress* vol. III (Ann Arbor: University of Michigan, 1975).

a. Children in Poverty

176. Poverty strikes some groups more severely than others. Perhaps most distressing is the growing number of children who are poor. Today one in every four American children under the age of six, and one in every two black children under six, are poor. The number of children in poverty rose by four million over the decade between 1973 and 1983, with the result that there are now more poor children in the United States than at any time since 1965.[31] The problem is particularly severe among female-headed families, where more than half of all children are poor. Two-thirds of black children and nearly three-quarters of Hispanic children in such families are poor.

177. Very many poor families with children receive no government assistance, have no health insurance, and cannot pay medical bills. Less than half are immunized against preventable diseases such as diphtheria and polio.[32] Poor children are disadvantaged even before birth; their mothers' lack of access to high quality prenatal care leaves them at much greater risk of premature birth, low-birth weight, physical and mental impairment, and death before their first birthday.

b. Women and Poverty

178. The past twenty years have witnessed a dramatic increase in the number of women in poverty.[33]

---

[31] Congressional Research Service and Congressional Budget Office, *Children in Poverty* (Washington, D.C., May 22, 1985), 57. This recent study also indicates that children are now the largest age group in poverty. We are the first industrialized nation in the world in which children are the poorest age group. See Daniel Patrick Moynihan, *Family and Nation* (New York: Harcourt, Brace, Jovanovich, 1986), 112.

[32] Children's Defense Fund, *American Children in Poverty* (Washington, D.C., 1984).

[33] This trend has been commonly referred to as the "feminization

This includes women raising children alone as well as women with inadequate income following divorce, widowhood, or retirement. More than one-third of all female-headed families are poor. Among minority families headed by women the poverty rate is over 50 percent.[34]

179. Wage discrimination against women is a major factor behind these high rates of poverty. Many women are employed but remain poor because their wages are too low. Women who work outside their homes full-time and year-round earn only 61 percent of what men earn. Thus, being employed full-time is not by itself a remedy for poverty among women. Hundreds of thousands of women hold full-time jobs but are still poor. Sixty percent of all women work in only ten occupations, and most new jobs for women are in areas with low pay and limited chances of advancement. Many women suffer discrimination in wages, salaries, job classifications, promotions, and other areas.[35] As a result, they find themselves in jobs that have low status, little security, weak unionization, and few fringe benefits. Such discrimination is immoral and efforts must be made to overcome the effects of sexism in our society.

180. Women's responsibilities for childrearing are another important factor to be considered. Despite the many changes in marriage and family life in recent decades, women continue to have primary respon-

---

of poverty." This term was coined by Dr. Diana Pierce in the *1980 Report to the President* of the National Advisory Council on Economic Opportunity to describe the dramatic increase in the proportion of the poor living in female-headed households.

[34] U.S. Bureau of the Census, Technical Paper 55, *Estimates of Poverty Including the Value of Non-Cash Benefits: 1984* (Washington, D.C., August 1985), 5, 23.

[35] Barbara Raskin and Heidi Hartmann, *Women's Work, Men's Work, Sex Segregation on the Job*, National Academy of Sciences (Washington, D.C.: National Academy Press, 1986), pp. 10–126.

sibility in this area. When marriages break up, mothers typically take custody of the children and bear the major financial responsibility for supporting them. Women often anticipate that they will leave the labor force to have and raise children, and often make job and career choices accordingly. In other cases they are not hired or promoted to higher paying jobs because of their childrearing responsibilities. In addition, most divorced or separated mothers do not get child support payments. In 1983, less than half of women raising children alone had been awarded child support, and of those, only half received the full amount to which they were entitled. Even fewer women (14 percent) are awarded alimony, and many older women are left in poverty after a lifetime of homemaking and childrearing.[36] Such women have great difficulty finding jobs and securing health insurance.

c. Racial Minorities and Poverty

181. Most poor people in our nation are white, but the rates of poverty in our nation are highest among those who have borne the brunt of racial prejudice and discrimination. For example, blacks are about three times more likely to be poor than whites. While one out of every nine white Americans is poor, one of every three blacks and Native Americans and more than one of every four Hispanics are poor.[37] While some members of minority communities have suc-

[36] U.S. Bureau of the Census, series P-23, no. 124, *Special Study Child Support and Alimony: 1981 Current Population Report* (Washington, D.C., 1981).

[37] U.S. House of Representatives Subcommittee on Oversight and Public Assistance and Unemployment Compensation, Committee on Ways and Means, *Background Material on Poverty* (Washington, D.C., October, 1983). See also Committee on Ways and Means, U.S. House of Representatives, *Children in Poverty*, 3.

cessfully moved up the economic ladder, the overall picture indicates that black family income is only 55 percent of white family income, reflecting an income gap that is wider now than at any time in the last fifteen years.[38]

182. Despite the gains which have been made toward racial equality, prejudice and discrimination in our own time as well as the effects of past discrimination continue to exclude many members of racial minorities from the mainstream of American life. Discriminatory practices in labor markets, in educational systems, and in electoral politics create major obstacles for blacks, Hispanics, Native Americans, and other racial minorities in their struggle to improve their economic status.[39] Such discrimination is evidence of the continuing presence of racism in our midst. In our pastoral letter, *Brothers and Sisters to Us*, we have described this racism as a sin—"a sin that divides the human family, blots out the image of God among specific members of that family, and violates the fundamental human dignity of those called to be children of the same Father."[40]

2. Economic Inequality

183. Important to our discussion of poverty in America is an understanding of the degree of economic inequality in our nation. Our economy is marked by a very uneven distribution of wealth and income. For example, it is estimated that 28 percent of the total net wealth is held by the richest 2 percent of families in the United States. The top ten percent holds 57

---

[38] The National Urban League, *The Status of Black America 1984* (New York, January 1984).

[39] Ibid.

[40] NCCB, *Brothers and Sisters to Us* Pastoral Letter on Racism in Our Day (Washington, D.C.: USCC Office of Publishing and Promotion Services, 1979).

percent of the net wealth.[41] If homes and other real estate are excluded, the concentration of ownership of "financial wealth" is even more glaring. In 1983, 54 percent of the total net financial assets were held by 2 percent of all families, those whose annual income is over $125,000. Eighty-six percent of these assets were held by the top 10 percent of all families.[42]

184. Although disparities in the distribution of income are less extreme, they are still striking. In 1984 the bottom 20 percent of American families received only 4.7 percent of the total income in the nation and the bottom 40 percent received only 15.7 percent, the lowest share on record in U.S. history. In contrast, the top one-fifth received 42.9 percent of the total income, the highest share since 1948.[43] These figures are only partial and very imperfect measures of the inequality in our society.[44] However, they do suggest that the degree of inequality is quite large. In comparison with other industrialized nations, the United States is among the more unequal in terms of income

---

[41] Federal Reserve Board, "Survey of Consumer Finances, 1983: A Second Report," reprint from the *Federal Reserve Bulletin* (Washington, D.C., December 1984), 857-868. This survey defines net worth as the difference between gross assets and gross liabilities. The survey's estimates include all financial assets, equity in homes and other real property, as well as all financial liabilities such as consumer credit and other debts.

[42] Ibid., 863-864.

[43] U.S. Bureau of the Census, series P-60, no. 149, 11.

[44] Income distribution figures give only a static picture of income shares. They do not reflect the significant movement of families into and out of different income categories over an extended period of time. See *Years of Poverty, Years of Plenty*, 13. It should also be noted that these figures reflect pre-tax incomes. However, since the national tax structure is proportional for a large segment of the population, it does not have a significant impact on the distribution of income. See Joseph Pechman, *Who Paid Taxes, 1966-85?* (Washington, D.C.: The Brookings Institution, 1985), 51.

distribution.[45] Moreover, the gap between rich and poor in our nation has increased during the last decade.[46] These inequities are of particular concern because they reflect the uneven distribution of power in our society. They suggest that the level of participation in the political and social spheres is also very uneven.

185. Catholic social teaching does not require absolute equality in the distribution of income and wealth. Some degree of inequality not only is acceptable, but also may be considered desirable for economic and social reasons, such as the need for incentives and the provision of greater rewards for greater risks. However, unequal distribution should be evaluated in terms of several moral principles we have enunciated: the priority of meeting the basic needs of the poor and the importance of increasing the level of participation by all members of society in the economic life of the nation. These norms establish a strong presumption against extreme inequality of income and wealth as long as there are poor, hungry, and homeless people in our midst. They also suggest that extreme inequalities are detrimental to the development of social solidarity and community. In view of these norms we find the disparities of income and wealth in the United States to be unacceptable. Justice requires that all members of our society work for economic, political, and social reforms that will decrease these inequities.

3. Guidelines for Action

186. Our recommendations for dealing with poverty in the United States build upon several moral

---

[45] Lars Osberg, *Economic Inequality in the United States* (New York: M. E. Sharpe, Inc., 1984), 24-28.

[46] U.S. Bureau of the Census, series P-60, no. 149, 11.

principles that were explored in chapter two of this letter. The themes of human dignity and the preferential option for the poor are at the heart of our approach; they compel us to confront the issue of poverty with a real sense of urgency.

187. The principle of social solidarity suggests that alleviating poverty will require fundamental changes in social and economic structures that perpetuate glaring inequalities and cut off millions of citizens from full participation in the economic and social life of the nation. The process of change should be one that draws together all citizens, whatever their economic status, into one community.

188. The principle of participation leads us to the conviction that the most appropriate and fundamental solutions to poverty will be those that enable people to take control of their own lives. For poverty is not merely the lack of adequate financial resources. It entails a more profound kind of deprivation, a denial of full participation in the economic, social, and political life of society and an inability to influence decisions that affect one's life. It means being powerless in a way that assaults not only one's pocketbook but also one's fundamental human dignity. Therefore, we should seek solutions that enable the poor to help themselves through such means as employment. Paternalistic programs which do too much *for* and too little *with* the poor are to be avoided.

189. The responsibility for alleviating the plight of the poor falls upon all members of society. As individuals, all citizens have a duty to assist the poor through acts of charity and personal commitment. But private charity and voluntary action are not sufficient. We also carry out our moral responsibility to assist and empower the poor by working collectively through government to establish just and effective public policies.

190. Although the task of alleviating poverty is complex and demanding, we should be encouraged by examples of our nation's past successes in this area. Our history shows that we can reduce poverty. During the 1960s and early 1970s, the official poverty rate was cut in half, due not only to a healthy economy, but also to public policy decisions that improved the nation's income transfer programs. It is estimated, for example, that in the late 1970s federal benefit programs were lifting out of poverty about 70 percent of those who would have otherwise been poor.[47]

191. During the last twenty-five years, the Social Security Program has dramatically reduced poverty among the elderly.[48] In addition, in 1983 it lifted out of poverty almost 1.5 million children of retired, deceased, and disabled workers.[49] Medicare has enhanced the life expectancy and health status of elderly and disabled people, and Medicaid has reduced infant mortality and greatly improved access to health care for the poor.[50]

---

[47] "Poverty in the United States: Where Do We Stand Now?" *Focus* (University of Wisconsin: Institute for Research on Poverty, Winter 1984). See also Danzinger and Gottschalk, "The Poverty of Losing Ground," *Challenge* 28:2 (May/June 1985). As these studies indicate, the slowing of the economy after 1969 tended to push more people into poverty, a trend that was offset to a great extent by the broadening of federal benefit programs. Likewise, the cutbacks in federal programs for the poor in recent years have contributed to the increase in poverty. For other analyses of the causes and cures of poverty see Charles Murray, *Losing Ground: American Social Policy 1950-1980* (New York: Basic Books, Inc., 1984); Ben J. Wattenberg, *The Good News Is the Bad News Is Wrong* (New York: Simon and Shuster, 1984); and Michael Harrington, *The New American Poverty* (New York: Holt, Rinehart, and Winston, 1984).

[48] *Family and Nation*, 111-113.

[49] Committee on Ways and Means, *Children In Poverty*. Calculation based on Tables 6-1 and 6-2, 180-181; and estimates of social insurance transfers on 221-222.

[50] Paul Starr, *The Social Transformation of American Medicine* (New York: Basic Books, Inc., 1982), 373.

192. These and other successful social welfare programs are evidence of our nation's commitment to social justice and a decent life for everyone. They also indicate that we have the capacity to design programs that are effective and provide necessary assistance to the needy in a way that respects their dignity. Yet it is evident that not all social welfare programs have been successful. Some have been ill-designed, ineffective, and wasteful. No one has been more aware of this than the poor themselves, who have suffered the consequences. Where programs have failed, we should discard them, learn from our mistakes, and fashion a better alternative. Where programs have succeeded, we should acknowledge that fact and build on those successes. In every instance, we must summon a new creativity and commitment to eradicate poverty in our midst and to guarantee all Americans their right to share in the blessings of our land.

193. Before discussing directions for reform in public policy, we must speak frankly about misunderstandings and stereotypes of the poor. For example, a common misconception is that most of the poor are racial minorities. In fact, about two-thirds of the poor are white.[51] It is also frequently suggested that people stay on welfare for many years, do not work, could work if they wanted to, and have children who will be on welfare. In fact, reliable data show that these are not accurate descriptions of most people who are poor and on welfare. Over a decade people move on and off welfare, and less than 1 percent obtain these benefits for all ten years.[52] Nor is it true that the rolls of Aid to Families with Dependent Children (AFDC) are filled with able-bodied adults who could but will not work. The majority of AFDC recipients are young

---

[51] U.S. Bureau of the Census, series P-60, no. 149, 11.
[52] *Years of Poverty, Years of Plenty,* 13.

children and their mothers who must remain at home.[53] These mothers are also accused of having more children so that they can raise their allowances. The truth is that 70 percent of AFDC families have only one or two children and that there is little financial advantage in having another. In a given year, almost half of all families who receive AFDC include an adult who has worked full or part-time.[54] Research has consistently demonstrated that people who are poor have the same strong desire to work that characterizes the rest of the population.[55]

194. We ask everyone to refrain from actions, words, or attitudes that stigmatize the poor, that exaggerate the benefits received by the poor, and that inflate the amount of fraud in welfare payments.[56] These are symptoms of a punitive attitude towards the poor. The belief persists in this country that the poor are poor by choice or through laziness, that anyone can escape poverty by hard work, and that welfare programs make it easier for people to avoid work. Thus, public attitudes toward programs for the poor tend to differ sharply from attitudes about other benefits and programs. Some of the most generous sub-

---

[53] Center on Social Welfare Policy and Law, *Beyond the Myths: The Families Helped by the AFDC Program* (New York, 1985).

[54] Ibid. This booklet cites Census Bureau data showing that in 1980 about 45% of those families who received AFDC also had earned income during that year, and that the average number of weeks worked during the year was 32.1.

[55] Leonard Goodwin, *Causes and Cures of Welfare* (Lexington, Mass.: Lexington Books, 1983), ch. 1. See also Leonard Goodwin, "Can Workfare Work?" *Public Welfare* 39 (Fall 1981): 19-25.

[56] *Beyond the Myths*. With respect to error and fraud rates in AFDC, this booklet notes that erroneous payments in the AFDC program account for less than 10% of the benefits paid. No more than 8.1% of the families on AFDC received overpayments as a result of client error. In less than 4.5% of all AFDC cases nationally are questions of fraud raised. Moreover, in over 40% of these cases, a review of the facts indicated that there was insufficient evidence to support an allegation of fraud.

sidies for individuals and corporations are taken for granted and are not even called benefits but entitlements.[57] In contrast, programs for the poor are called handouts and receive a great deal of critical attention, even though they account for less than 10 percent of the federal budget.[58]

195. We now wish to propose several elements which we believe are necessary for a national strategy to deal with poverty. We offer this not as a comprehensive list but as an invitation for others to join the discussion and take up the task of fighting poverty.

196. a. *The first line of attack against poverty must be to build and sustain a healthy economy that provides employment opportunities at just wages for all adults who are able to work.* Poverty is intimately linked to the issue of employment. Millions are poor because they have lost their jobs or because their wages are too low. The persistent high levels of unemployment during the last decade are a major reason why poverty has increased in recent years.[59] Expanded employment especially in the private sector would promote human dignity, increase social solidarity, and promote self-reliance of the poor. It should also reduce the need for welfare programs and generate the income necessary to support those who remain in need and cannot work: elderly, disabled, and chronically ill people, and single parents of young children. It should also be recognized that the persistence of poverty harms the larger society because the depressed purchasing power of the poor contributes to the periodic cycles of stagnation in the economy.

---

[57] P. G. Peterson, "No More Free Lunch for the Middle Class," *New York Times Magazine* (January 17, 1982).

[58] Interfaith Action for Economic Justice, *End Results: The Impact of Federal Policies Since 1980 on Low-Income Americans* (Washington, D.C.), 2.

[59] "The Poverty of Losing Ground," 32-38.

197. In recent years the minimum wage has not been adjusted to keep pace with inflation. Its real value has declined by 24 percent since 1981. We believe Congress should raise the minimum wage in order to restore some of the purchasing power it has lost due to inflation.

198. While job creation and just wages are major elements of a national strategy against poverty, they are clearly not enough. Other more specific policies are necessary to remedy the institutional causes of poverty and to provide for those who cannot work.

199. b. *Vigorous action should be undertaken to remove barriers to full and equal employment for women and minorities.* Too many women and minorities are locked into jobs with low pay, poor working conditions, and little opportunity for career advancement. So long as we tolerate a situation in which people can work full-time and still be below the poverty line—a situation common among those earning the minimum wage—too many will continue to be counted among the "working poor." Concerted efforts must be made through job training, affirmative action, and other means to assist those now prevented from obtaining more lucrative jobs. Action should also be taken to upgrade poorer paying jobs and to correct wage differentials that discriminate unjustly against women.

200. c. *Self-help efforts among the poor should be fostered by programs and policies in both the private and public sectors.* We believe that an effective way to attack poverty is through programs that are small in scale, locally based, and oriented toward empowering the poor to become self-sufficient. Corporations, private organizations, and the public sector can provide seed money, training and technical assistance, and organizational support for self-help projects in a wide variety of areas such as low-income housing, credit unions, worker cooperatives, legal assistance, and neighborhood and community organizations. Efforts that enable the poor

to participate in the ownership and control of economic resources are especially important.

201. Poor people must be empowered to take charge of their own futures and become responsible for their own economic advancement. Personal motivation and initiative, combined with social reform, are necessary elements to assist individuals in escaping poverty. By taking advantage of opportunities for education, employment, and training, and by working together for change, the poor can help themselves to be full participants in our economic, social, and political life.

202. d. *The tax system should be continually evaluated in terms of its impact on the poor.* This evaluation should be guided by three principles. First, the tax system should raise adequate revenues to pay for the public needs of society, especially to meet the basic needs of the poor. Secondly, the tax system should be structured according to the principle of progressivity, so that those with relatively greater financial resources pay a higher rate of taxation. The inclusion of such a principle in tax policies is an important means of reducing the severe inequalities of income and wealth in the nation. Action should be taken to reduce or offset the fact that most sales taxes and payroll taxes place a disproportionate burden on those with lower incomes. Thirdly, families below the official poverty line should not be required to pay income taxes. Such families are, by definition, without sufficient resources to purchase the basic necessities of life. They should not be forced to bear the additional burden of paying income taxes.[60]

203. e. *All of society should make a much stronger commitment to education for the poor.* Any long-term solution to poverty in this country must pay serious attention

---

[60] The tax reform legislation of 1986 did a great deal to achieve this goal. It removed from the federal income tax rolls virtually all families below the official poverty line.

to education, public and private, in school and out of school. Lack of adequate education, especially in the inner city setting, prevents many poor people from escaping poverty. In addition, illiteracy, a problem that affects tens of millions of Americans, condemns many to joblessness or chronically low wages. Moreover, it excludes them in many ways from sharing in the political and spiritual life of the community.[61] Since poverty is fundamentally a problem of powerlessness and marginalization, the importance of education as a means of overcoming it cannot be overemphasized.

204. Working to improve education in our society is an investment in the future, an investment that should include both the public and private school systems. Our Catholic schools have the well-merited reputation of providing excellent education, especially for the poor. Catholic inner-city schools provide an otherwise unavailable educational alternative for many poor families. They provide one effective vehicle for disadvantaged students to lift themselves out of poverty. We commend the work of all those who make great sacrifices to maintain these inner-city schools. We pledge ourselves to continue the effort to make Catholic schools models of education for the poor.

205. We also wish to affirm our strong support for the public school system in the United States. There can be no substitute for quality education in public schools, for that is where the large majority of all students, including Catholic students, are educated. In Catholic social teaching, basic education is a fundamental human right.[62] In our society a strong public school system is essential if we are to protect that right and allow everyone to develop to their maximum ability. Therefore, we strongly endorse the recent calls

---

[61] Jonathan Kozol, *Illiterate America* (New York: Anchor Press/Doubleday, 1985).

[62] *Peace on Earth*, 13.

for improvements in and support for public education, including improving the quality of teaching and enhancing the rewards for the teaching profession.[63] At all levels of education we need to improve the ability of our institutions to provide the personal and technical skills that are necessary for participation not only in today's labor market but also in contemporary society.

206. f. *Policies and programs at all levels should support the strength and stability of families, especially those adversely affected by the economy.* As a nation, we need to examine all aspects of economic life and assess their effects on families. Employment practices, health insurance policies, income security programs, tax policy, and service programs can either support or undermine the abilities of families to fulfill their roles in nurturing children and caring for infirm and dependent family members.

207. We affirm the principle enunciated by John Paul II that society's institutions and policies should be structured so that mothers of young children are not forced by economic necessity to leave their chil-

---

[63] These reports and studies include: E. Boyer, *High School: A Report on Secondary Education in America* (Princeton: Carnegie Foundation for the Advancement of Teaching, 1983); P. Cusick, *The American High School and the Egalitarian Ideal* (New York: Longman, 1983); J. I. Goodlad, *A Place Called School: Prospects for the Future* (New York: McGraw-Hill, 1983); The National Commission on Excellence in Education, *A Nation at Risk: The Imperative for Educational Reform* (Washington, D.C.: U.S. Department of Education, 1983); D. Ravitch, *The Troubled Crusade: American Education, 1945-1980* (New York: Basic Books, 1983); T. R. Sizer, *Horace's Compromise: The Dilemma of the American High School* (Boston: Houghton Mifflin, 1984); Task Force on Education for Economic Growth, *Action for Excellence: A Comprehensive Plan to Improve our Nation's Schools* (Denver: Education Commission of the States, 1983); and The Twentieth Century Fund Task Force on Federal Elementary and Secondary Education Policy, *Making the Grade* (New York: Twentieth Century Fund, 1983). For a discussion of the issues raised in these reports see *Harvard Educational Review* 54:1 (February 1984): 1-31.

dren for jobs outside the home.[64] The nation's social welfare and tax policies should support parents' decisions to care for their own children and should recognize the work of parents in the home because of its value for the family and for society.

208. For those children whose parents do work outside the home, there is a serious shortage of affordable, quality day care. Employers, governments, and private agencies need to improve both the availability and the quality of child care services. Likewise, families could be assisted by the establishment of parental leave policies that would assure job security for new parents.

209. The high rate of divorce and the alarming extent of teenage pregnancies in our nation are distressing signs of the breakdown of traditional family values. These destructive trends are present in all sectors of society: rich and poor; white, black, and brown; urban and rural. However, for the poor they tend to be more visible and to have more damaging economic consequences. These destructive trends must be countered by a revived sense of personal responsibility and commitment to family values.

210. g. *A thorough reform of the nation's welfare and income-support programs should be undertaken.* For millions of poor Americans the only economic safety net is the public welfare system. The programs that make up this system should serve the needs of the poor in a manner that respects their dignity and provides adequate support. In our judgment the present welfare system does not adequately meet these criteria.[65] We

---

[64] The Vatican, *Charter of the Rights of the Family* (Washington, D.C.: USCC Office of Publishing and Promotion Services, 1983). See also *On Human Work,* 19; *Familiaris Consortio,* 23, 81; and "Christian Solidarity Leads to Action," Address to Austrian Workers (Vienna, September 1983) in *Origins* 13:16 (September 29, 1983): 275.

[65] H. R. Rodgers, Jr., *The Cost of Human Neglect: America's Welfare* (Armonk, N.Y.: W. E. Sharpe, Inc., 1982); C. T. Waxman, *The Stigma*

believe that several improvements can and should be made within the framework of existing welfare programs. However, in the long run, more far-reaching reforms that go beyond the present system will be necessary. Among the immediate improvements that could be made are the following:

211. (1) *Public assistance programs should be designed to assist recipients, wherever possible, to become self-sufficient through gainful employment.* Individuals should not be worse off economically when they get jobs than when they rely only on public assistance. Under current rules, people who give up welfare benefits to work in low-paying jobs soon lose their Medicaid benefits. To help recipients become self-sufficient and reduce dependency on welfare, public assistance programs should work in tandem with job creation programs that include provisions for training, counseling, placement, and child care. Jobs for recipients of public assistance should be fairly compensated so that workers receive the full benefits and status associated with gainful employment.

212. (2) *Welfare programs should provide recipients with adequate levels of support.* This support should cover basic needs in food, clothing, shelter, health care, and other essentials. At present only 4 percent of poor families with children receive enough cash welfare benefits to lift them out of poverty.[66] The combined benefits of AFDC and food stamps typically come to less than three-fourths of the official poverty level.[67]

---

of Poverty, second edition (New York: Pergamon Press, 1983), especially ch. 5; and S. A. Levitan and C. M. Johnson, *Beyond the Safety Net: Reviving the Promise of Opportunity in America* (Cambridge, Mass.: Ballinger, 1984).

[66] *Children in Poverty.*

[67] U.S. House of Representatives Committee on Ways and Means, *Background Materials and Data on Programs Within the Jurisdiction of the Committee on Ways and Means* (Washington, D.C., February 22, 1985), 345-346.

Those receiving public assistance should not face the prospect of hunger at the end of the month, homelessness, sending children to school in ragged clothing, or inadequate medical care.

213. (3) *National eligibility standards and a national minimum benefit level for public assistance programs should be established.* Currently welfare eligibility and benefits vary greatly among states. In 1985 a family of three with no earnings had a maximum AFDC benefit of $96 a month in Mississippi and $558 a month in Vermont.[68] To remedy these great disparities, which are far larger than the regional differences in the cost of living, and to assure a floor of benefits for all needy people, our nation should establish and fund national minimum benefit levels and eligibility standards in cash assistance programs.[69] The benefits should also be indexed to reflect changes in the cost of living. These changes reflect standards that our nation has already put in place for aged and disabled people and veterans. Is it not possible to do the same for the children and their mothers who receive public assistance?

214. (4) *Welfare programs should be available to two-parent as well as single-parent families.* Most states now limit participation in AFDC to families headed by single parents, usually women.[70] The coverage of this program should be extended to two-parent families so that fathers who are unemployed or poorly paid do not have to leave home in order for their children

---

[68] Ibid., 347-348.

[69] In 1982, similar recommendations were made by eight former Secretaries of Health, Education, and Welfare (now Health and Human Services). In a report called "Welfare Policy in the United States," they suggested a number of ways in which national minimal standards might be set and strongly urged the establishment of a floor for all states and territories.

[70] Committee on Ways and Means, *Background Materials and Data on Programs.*

to receive help. Such a change would be a significant step toward strengthening two-parent families who are poor.

4. Conclusion

215. The search for a more human and effective way to deal with poverty should not be limited to short-term reform measures. The agenda for public debate should also include serious discussion of more fundamental alternatives to the existing welfare system. We urge that proposals for a family allowance or a children's allowance be carefully examined as a possible vehicle for ensuring a floor of income support for all children and their families.[71] Special attention is needed to develop new efforts that are targeted on long-term poverty, which has proven to be least responsive to traditional social welfare programs. The "negative income tax" is another major policy proposal that deserves continued discussion.[72] These and other proposals should be part of a creative and ongoing effort to fashion a system of income support for the poor that protects their basic dignity and provides the necessary assistance in a just and effective manner.

---

[71] France adopted a "family" or "children's" allowance in 1932, followed by Italy in 1936, The Netherlands in 1939, the United Kingdom in 1945, and Sweden in 1947. Arnold Heidenheimer, Hugh Heclo, and Carolyn Teich Adams, *Comparative Public Policy: The Politics of Social Choice in Europe and America* (New York: St. Martin's Press, 1975), 189, 199. See Also Robert Kuttner, *The Economic Illusion* (Boston: Houghton Mifflin Co., 1984), 243-246; and Joseph Piccione, *Help for Families on the Front Lines: The Theory and Practice of Family Allowances* (Washington, D.C.: The Free Congress Research and Education Foundation, 1983).

[72] Milton Friedman, *Capitalism and Freedom* (University of Chicago Press, 1962), 190-195.

C. Food and Agriculture

216. The fundamental test of an economy is its ability to meet the essential human needs of this generation and future generations in an equitable fashion. Food, water, and energy are essential to life; their abundance in the United States has tended to make us complacent. But these goods—the foundation of God's gift of life—are too crucial to be taken for granted. God reminded the people of Israel that "the land is mine; for you are strangers and guests with me" (Lv 25:23, RSV). Our Christian faith calls us to contemplate God's creative and sustaining action and to measure our own collaboration with the Creator in using the earth's resources to meet human needs. While Catholic social teaching on the care of the environment and the management of natural resources is still in the process of development, a Christian moral perspective clearly gives weight and urgency to their use in meeting human needs.

217. No aspect of this concern is more pressing than the nation's food system. We are concerned that this food system may be in jeopardy as increasing numbers of farm bankruptcies and foreclosures result in increased concentration of land ownership.[73] We are likewise concerned about the increasing damage to natural resources resulting from many modern agricultural practices: the overconsumption of water, the depletion of topsoil, and the pollution of land and water. Finally, we are concerned about the stark reality of world hunger in spite of food surpluses. Our food production system is clearly in need of evaluation and reform.

---

[73] *The Current Financial Condition of Farmers and Farm Lenders*, Ag. Info. Bulletin no. 490 (Washington, D.C.: U.S. Department of Agriculture Economic Research Service, March 1985), viii-x.

1. U.S. Agriculture—Past and Present

218. The current crisis has to be assessed in the context of the vast diversity of U.S. crops and climates. For example, subsistence farming in Appalachia, where so much of the land is absentee-owned and where coal mining and timber production are the major economic interests, has little in common with family farm grain production in the central Midwest or ranching in the Great Plains. Likewise, large-scale irrigated fruit, vegetable, and cotton production in the central valley of California is very different from dairy farming in Wisconsin or tobacco and peanut production in the Southeast.

219. Two aspects of the complex history of U.S. land and food policy are particularly relevant. First, the United States entered this century with the ownership of productive land widely distributed. The Preemption Acts of the early 19th century and the Homestead Act of 1862 were an important part of that history. Wide distribution of ownership was reflected in the number and decentralization of farms in the United States, a trend that reached its peak in the 1930s. The U.S. farm system included nearly 7 million owner-operators in 1935.[74] By 1983 the number of U.S. farms had declined to 2.4 million, and only about 3 percent of the population were engaged in producing food.[75] Second, U.S. food policy has had a parallel goal of keeping the consumer cost of food low. As a result, Americans today spend less of their disposable income on food than people in any other industrialized country.[76]

---

[74] Data on farms and farm population are drawn from *Agricultural Statistics*, annual reports of the U.S. Department of Agriculture, Washington, D.C.

[75] Irma T. Elo and Calvin L. Beale, *Rural Development, Poverty, and Natural Resources* (Washington, D.C.: National Center for Food and Agricultural Policy, Resources for the Future, 1985).

[76] *National Food Review*, USDA, no. 29 (Winter/Spring 1985). In

220. These outcomes require scrutiny. First of all, the loss of farms and the exodus of farmers from the land have led to the loss of a valued way of life, the decline of many rural communities, and the increased concentration of land ownership. Secondly, while low food prices benefit consumers who are left with additional income to spend on other goods, these pricing policies put pressure on farmers to increase output and hold down costs. This has led them to replace human labor with cheaper energy, expand farm size to employ new technologies favoring larger scale operations, neglect soil and water conservation, underpay farmworkers, and oppose farmworker unionization.[77]

221. Today nearly half of U.S. food production comes from the 4 percent of farms with over $200,000 in gross sales.[78] Many of these largest farms are no longer operated by families, but by managers hired by owners.[79] Nearly three-quarters of all farms, accounting for only 13 percent of total farm sales, are comparatively small. They are often run by part-time farmers who derive most of their income from off-farm employment. The remaining 39 percent of sales comes from the 24 percent of farms grossing between $40,000 and $200,000. It is this group of farmers, located throughout the country and caught up in the

1984 Americans were spending 15.1% of their disposable income on food. This is an average figure. Many low-income people spent a good deal more and others much less.

[77] Luther Tweeten, *Causes and Consequences of Structural Change in the Farming Industry* (Washington, D.C.: National Planning Association, 1984), 7.

[78] *Economic Indicators of the Farm Sector: Income and Balance Sheet Statistics, 1983*, ECIFS 3-3 (Washington, D.C.: U.S. Department of Agriculture Economic Research Service, September 1984).

[79] Marion Clawson, *Ownership Patterns of Natural Resources in America: Implications for Distribution of Wealth and Income* (Washington, D.C.: Resources for the Future, Summer 1983).

long-term trend toward fewer and larger farms, who are at the center of the present farm crisis.

222. During the 1970s new markets for farm exports created additional opportunities for profit and accelerated the industrialization of agriculture, a process already stimulated by new petroleum-based, large-scale technologies that allowed farmers to cultivate many more acres. Federal tax policies and farm programs fostered this tendency by encouraging too much capital investment in agriculture and overemphasizing large-scale technologies.[80] The results were greater production, increases in the value of farmland, and heavy borrowing to finance expansion. In the 1980s, with export markets shrinking and commodity prices and land values declining, many farmers cannot repay their loans.

223. Their situation has been aggravated by certain "external" factors: persistent high interest rates that make it difficult to repay or refinance loans, the heavy debt burden of food-deficient countries, the high value of the dollar, dramatically higher U.S. budget and trade deficits, and generally reduced international trade following the worldwide recession of the early 1980s. The United States is unlikely to recapture its former share of the world food and fiber trade, and it is not necessarily an appropriate goal to attempt to do so. Exports are not the solution to U.S. farm problems. Past emphasis on producing for overseas markets has contributed to the strain on our natural resource base and has also undermined the efforts of many less developed countries in attaining self-reliance in feeding their own people. In attempting to correct these abuses, however, we must not reduce our capability to help meet emergency food needs.

---

[80] *Causes and Consequences*, 7; and *A Time to Choose: Summary Report on the Structure of Agriculture* (Washington, D.C.: U.S. Department of Agriculture, January 1981).

224. Some farmers face financial insolvency because of their own eagerness to take advantage of what appeared to be favorable investment opportunities. This was partly in response to the encouragement of public policy incentives and the advice of economists and financiers. Nevertheless, farmers should share some responsibility for their current plight.

225. Four other aspects of the current situation concern us: first, land ownership is becoming further concentrated as units now facing bankruptcy are added to existing farms and nonfarm corporations. Diversity of ownership and widespread participation are declining in this sector of the economy as they have in others. Since differing scales of operation and the investment of family labor have been important for American farm productivity, this increasing concentration of ownership in almost all sectors of agriculture points to an important change in that system.[81] Of particular concern is the growing phenomenon of "vertical integration" whereby companies gain control of two or three of the links in the food chain: as suppliers of farm inputs, landowners, and food processors. This increased concentration could also adversely affect food prices.

226. Second, diversity and richness in American society are lost as farm people leave the land and rural communities decay. It is not just a question of coping with additional unemployment and a need for retraining and relocation. It is also a matter of maintaining opportunities for employment and human

---

[81] The nature of this transformation and its implications have been addressed previously by the USCC Committee on Social Development and World Peace in a February 1979 statement *The Family Farm* and again in May 1980 by the bishops of the Midwest in a joint pastoral letter *Strangers and Guests: Toward Community in the Heartland.*

development in a variety of economic sectors and cultural contexts.

227. Third, although the United States has set a world standard for food production, it has not done so without cost to our natural resource base.[82] On nearly one-quarter of our most productive cropland, topsoil erosion currently exceeds the rate at which it can be replaced by natural processes. Similarly, underground water supplies are being depleted in areas where food production depends on irrigation. Furthermore, chemical fertilizers, pesticides, and herbicides, considered now almost essential to today's agriculture, pollute the air, water, and soil, and pose countless health hazards. Finally, where the expansion of residential, industrial, and recreational areas makes it rewarding to do so, vast acreages of prime farmland, three million acres per year by some estimates, are converted to nonfarm use. The continuation of these practices, reflecting short-term investment interests or immediate income needs of farmers and other landowners, constitutes a danger to future food production because these practices are not sustainable.

228. Farm owners and farmworkers are the immediate stewards of the natural resources required to produce the food that is necessary to sustain life. These resources must be understood as gifts of a generous God. When they are seen in that light and when the human race is perceived as a single moral community, we gain a sense of the substantial responsibility we bear as a nation for the world food system. Meeting

---

[82] *Soil Conservation in America: What Do We Have To Lose?* (Washington, D.C.: American Farmland Trust, 1984); E. Philip LeVeen, "Domestic Food Security and Increasing Competition for Water," in Lawrence Busch and William B. Lacy, eds., *Food Security in the United States* (Boulder, Colo.: Westview Press, 1984), 52. See also *America's Soil and Water: Condition and Trends* (Washington, D.C.: U.S. Department of Agriculture Soil Conservation Service, 1981).

111

human needs today and in the future demands an increased sense of stewardship and conservation from owners, managers, and regulators of all resources, especially those required for the production of food.

229. Fourth, the situation of racial minorities in the U.S. food system is a matter of special pastoral concern. They are largely excluded from significant participation in the farm economy. Despite the agrarian heritage of so many Hispanics, for example, they operate only a minute fraction of America's farms.[83] Black-owned farms, at one time a significant resource for black participation in the economy, have been disappearing at a dramatic rate in recent years,[84] a trend that the U.S. Commission on Civil Rights has warned "can only serve to further diminish the stake of blacks in the social order and reinforce their skepticism regarding the concept of equality under the law."[85]

230. It is largely as hired farm laborers rather than farm owners that minorities participate in the farm economy. Along with many white farmworkers, they are, by and large, the poorest paid and least benefited of any laboring group in the country. Moreover, they are not as well protected by law and public policy as other groups of workers; and their efforts to organize and bargain collectively have been systematically and vehemently resisted, usually by farmers themselves. Migratory field workers are particularly susceptible to exploitation. This is reflected not only in their characteristically low wages but also in the low standards of housing, health care, and education made available to these workers and their families.[86]

---

[83] *1982 Census of Agriculture*.

[84] U.S. Commission on Civil Rights, *The Decline of Black Farming in America* (Washington, D.C.: U.S. Commission on Civil Rights, February 1982), esp. 65-69 regarding their property.

[85] Ibid., 8.

[86] U.S. Department of Labor, *Hearings Concerning Proposed Full Sanitation Standards*, document no. H-308 (Washington, D.C., 1984).

2. Guidelines for Action

231. We are convinced that current trends in the food sector are not in the best interests of the United States or of the global community. The decline in the number of moderate-sized farms, increased concentration of land ownership, and the mounting evidence of poor resource conservation raise serious questions of morality and public policy. As pastors, we cannot remain silent while thousands of farm families caught in the present crisis lose their homes, their land, and their way of life. We approach this situation, however, aware that it reflects longer-term conditions that carry consequences for the food system as a whole and for the resources essential for food production.

232. While much of the change needed must come from the cooperative efforts of farmers themselves, we strongly believe that there is an important role for public policy in the protection of dispersed ownership through family farms, as well as in the preservation of natural resources. We suggest three guidelines for both public policy and private efforts aimed at shaping the future of American agriculture.

233. *First, moderate-sized farms operated by families on a full-time basis should be preserved and their economic viability protected.* Similarly, small farms and part-time farming, particularly in areas close to cities, should be encouraged. As we have noted elsewhere in this pastoral letter,[87] there is genuine social and economic value in maintaining a wide distribution in the ownership of productive property. The democratization of decision making and control of the land resulting from wide distribution of farm ownership are protections against concentration of power and a consequent possible loss of responsiveness to public need in this

---

[87] Ch. II, para. 112.

crucial sector of the economy.[88] Moreover, when those who work in an enterprise also share in its ownership, their active commitment to the purpose of the endeavor and their participation in it are enhanced. Ownership provides incentives for diligence and is a source of an increased sense that the work being done is one's own. This is particularly significant in a sector as vital to human well-being as agriculture.

234. Furthermore, diversity in farm ownership tends to prevent excessive consumer dependence on business decisions that seek maximum return on invested capital, thereby making the food system overly susceptible to fluctuations in the capital markets. This is particularly relevant in the case of nonfarm corporations that enter agriculture in search of high profits. If the return drops substantially, or if it appears that better profits can be obtained by investing elsewhere, the corporation may cut back or even close down operations without regard to the impact on the community or on the food system in general. In similar circumstances full-time farmers, with a heavy personal investment in their farms and strong ties to the community, are likely to persevere in the hope of better times. Family farms also make significant economic and social contributions to the life of rural communities.[89] They support farm suppliers and other local merchants, and their farms support the tax base needed to pay for roads, schools, and other vital services.

235. This rural interdependence has value beyond the rural community itself. Both Catholic social teaching and the traditions of our country have emphasized the importance of maintaining the rich plurality of social institutions that enhances personal freedom and

---

[88] *A Time to Choose,* 148.

[89] Luther Tweeten, "The Economics of Small Farms," *Science* vol. 219 (March 4, 1983): 1041.

increases the opportunity for participation in community life. Movement toward a smaller number of very large farms employing wage workers would be a movement away from this institutional pluralism. By contributing to the vitality of rural communities, full-time residential farmers enrich the social and political life of the nation as a whole. Cities, too, benefit soundly and economically from a vibrant rural economy based on family farms. Because of out-migration of farm and rural people, too much of this enriching diversity has been lost already.

236. *Second, the opportunity to engage in farming should be protected as a valuable form of work.* At a time when unemployment in the country is already too high, any unnecessary increase in the number of unemployed people, however small, should be avoided. Farm unemployment leads to further rural unemployment as rural businesses lose their customers and close down. The loss of people from the land also entails the loss of expertise in farm and land management and creates a need for retraining and relocating another group of displaced workers.

237. Losing any job is painful, but losing one's farm and having to leave the land can be tragic. It often means the sacrifice of a family heritage and a way of life. Once farmers sell their land and their equipment, their move is practically irreversible. The costs of returning are so great that few who leave ever come back. Even the small current influx of people into agriculture attracted by lower land values will not balance this loss. Society should help those who would and could continue effectively in farming.

238. *Third, effective stewardship of our natural resources should be a central consideration in any measures regarding U.S. agriculture.* Such stewardship is a contribution to the common good that is difficult to assess in purely economic terms, because it involves the care of resources entrusted to us by our Creator for the

benefit of all. Responsibility for the stewardship of these resources rests on society as a whole. Since farmers make their living from the use of this endowment, however, they bear a particular obligation to be caring stewards of soil and water. They fulfill this obligation by participating in soil and water conservation programs, using farm practices that enhance the quality of the resources, and maintaining prime farmland in food production rather than letting it be converted to nonfarm uses.

3. Policies and Actions

239. The human suffering involved in the present situation and the long-term structural changes occurring in this sector call for responsible action by the whole society. A half-century of federal farm-price supports, subsidized credit, production-oriented research and extension services, and special tax policies for farmers have made the federal government a central factor in almost every aspect of American agriculture.[90] No redirection of current trends can occur without giving close attention to these programs.

240. A prime consideration in all agricultural trade and food assistance policies should be the contribution our nation can make to global food security. This means continuing and increasing food aid without depressing Third World markets or using food as a weapon in international politics. It also means not subsidizing exports in ways that lead to trade wars and instability in international food markets.

241. We offer the following suggestions for governmental action with regard to the farm and food sector of the economy.

---

[90] U.S. Department of Agriculture, *History of Agricultural Price-Support and Adjustment Programs, 1933-1984*, Ag. Info. Bulletin no. 485 (Washington, D.C.: U.S. Department of Agriculture Economic Research Service, December 1984).

242. a. The current crisis calls for special measures to assist otherwise viable family farms that are threatened with bankruptcy or foreclosure. Operators of such farms should have access to emergency credit, reduced rates of interest, and programs of debt restructuring. Rural lending institutions facing problems because of nonpayment or slow payment of large farm loans should also have access to temporary assistance. Farmers, their families, and their communities will gain immediately from these and other short-term measures aimed at keeping these people on the land.

243. b. Established federal farm programs, whose benefits now go disproportionately to the largest farmers,[91] should be reassessed for their long-term effects on the structure of agriculture. Income-support programs that help farmers according to the amount of food they produce or the number of acres they farm should be subject to limits that ensure a fair income to all farm families and should restrict participation to producers who genuinely need such income assistance. There should also be a strict ceiling on price-support payments which assist farmers in times of falling prices, so that benefits go to farms of moderate or small size. To succeed in redirecting the benefits of these programs while holding down costs to the public, consideration should be given to a broader application of mandatory production control programs.[92]

244. c. We favor reform of tax policies which now encourage the growth of large farms, attract invest-

---

[91] *The Distribution of Benefits from the 1982 Federal Crop Programs* (Washington, D.C.: U.S. Senate Committee on the Budget, November 1984).

[92] "The Great Debate on Mandatory Production Controls" in *Farm Policy Perspectives: Setting the Stage for 1985 Agricultural Legislation* (Washington, D.C.: U.S. Senate Committee on Agriculture, Nutrition, and Forestry, April 1984).

ments into agriculture by nonfarmers seeking tax shelters, and inequitably benefit large and well-financed farming operations.[93] Offsetting nonfarm income with farm "losses" has encouraged high-income investors to acquire farm assets with no intention of depending on them for a living as family farmers must. The ability to depreciate capital equipment faster than its actual decline in value has benefited wealthy investors and farmers. Lower tax rates on capital gains have stimulated farm expansion and larger investments in energy-intensive equipment and technologies as substitutes for labor. Changes in estate tax laws have consistently favored the largest estates. All of these results have demonstrated that reassessment of these and similar tax provisions is needed.[94] We continue, moreover, to support a progressive land tax on farm acreage to discourage the accumulation of excessively large holdings.[95]

245. d. Although it is often assumed that farms must grow in size in order to make the most efficient and productive use of sophisticated and costly technologies, numerous studies have shown that medium-sized commercial farms achieve most of the technical cost efficiencies available in agriculture today. We, therefore, recommend that the research and extension resources of the federal government and the nation's land grant colleges and universities be redirected toward improving the productivity of small and medium-sized farms.[96]

---

[93] *A Time to Choose*, 91.

[94] Richard Dunford, *The Effects of Federal Income Tax Policy on U.S. Agriculture* (Washington, D.C.: Subcommittee on Agriculture and Transportation of the Joint Economic Committee of the Congress of the United States, December 21, 1984).

[95] This proposal was put forward thirteen years ago in *Where Shall the People Live? A Special Message of the United States Catholic Bishops* (Washington, D.C.: USCC Office of Publishing and Promotion Services, 1972).

[96] Thomas E. Miller, et al., *Economies of Size in U.S. Field Crop*

118

246. e. Since soil and water conservation, like other efforts to protect the environment, are contributions to the good of the whole society, it is appropriate for the public to bear a share of the cost of these practices and to set standards for environmental protection. Government should, therefore, encourage farmers to adopt more conserving practices and distribute the costs of this conservation more broadly.

247. f. Justice demands that worker guarantees and protections such as minimum wages and benefits and unemployment compensation be extended to hired farmworkers on the same basis as all other workers. There is also an urgent need for additional farmworker housing, health care, and educational assistance.

4. Solidarity in the Farm Community

248. While there is much that government can and should do to change the direction of farm and food policy in this country, that change in direction also depends upon the cooperation and good will of farmers. The incentives in our farm system to take risks, to expand farm size, and to speculate in farmland values are great. Hence, farmers and ranchers must weigh these incentives against the values of family, rural community, care of the soil, and a food system responsive to long-term as well as short-term food needs of the nation and the world. The ever present temptation to individualism and greed must be countered by a determined movement toward solidarity in the farm community. Farmers should approach farming in a cooperative way, working with other farmers in the purchase of supplies and equipment and in the marketing of produce. It is not necessary for every farmer to be in competition against every other farmer.

Farming (Washington, D.C.: U.S. Department of Agriculture Economic Research Service, July 1981).

Such cooperation can be extended to the role farmers play through their various general and community organizations in shaping and implementing governmental farm and food policies.[97] Likewise, it is possible to seek out and adopt technologies that reduce costs and enhance productivity without demanding increases in farm size. New technologies are not forced on farmers; they are chosen by farmers themselves.

249. Farmers also must end their opposition to farmworker unionization efforts. Farmworkers have a legitimate right to belong to unions of their choice and to bargain collectively for just wages and working conditions. In pursuing that right they are protecting the value of labor in agriculture, a protection that also applies to farmers who devote their own labor to their farm operations.

5. Conclusion

250. The U.S. food system is an integral part of the larger economy of the nation and the world. As such this integral role necessitates the cooperation of rural and urban interests in resolving the challenges and problems facing agriculture. The very nature of agricultural enterprise and the family farm traditions of this country have kept it a highly competitive sector with a widely dispersed ownership of the most fundamental input to production, the land. That competitive, diverse structure, proven to be a dependable source of nutritious and affordable food for this country and millions of people in other parts of the world, is now threatened. The food necessary for life, the land and water resources needed to produce that food, and the way of life of the people who make the land productive are at risk. Catholic social and ethical traditions attribute moral significance to each of these.

---

[97] See ch. IV.

120

Our response to the present situation should reflect a sensitivity to that moral significance, a determination that the United States will play its appropriate role in meeting global food needs, and a commitment to bequeath to future generations an enhanced natural environment and the same ready access to the necessities of life that most of us enjoy today. To farmers and farm workers who are suffering because of the farm crisis, we promise our solidarity, prayers, counseling and the other spiritual resources of our Catholic faith.

D. The U.S. Economy and the Developing Nations: Complexity, Challenge, and Choices

1. The Complexity of Economic Relations in an Interdependent World

251. The global economy is made up of national economies of industrialized countries of the North and the developing countries of the South, together with the network of economic relations that link them. It constitutes the framework in which the solidarity we seek on a national level finds its international expression. Traditional Catholic teaching on this global interdependence emphasizes the dignity of the human person, the unity of the human family, the universally beneficial purpose of the goods of the earth, the need to pursue the international common good, as well as the good of each nation, and the imperative of distributive justice. The United States plays a leading role in the international economic system, and we are concerned that U.S. relations with all nations—Can-

ada, Europe, Japan, and our other trading partners, as well as the socialist countries—reflect this teaching and be marked by fairness and mutual respect.

252. Nevertheless, without in the least discounting the importance of these linkages, our emphasis on the preferential option for the poor moves us to focus our attention mainly on U.S. relations with the Third World. Unless conscious steps are taken toward protecting human dignity and fostering human solidarity in these relationships, we can look forward to increased conflict and inequity, threatening the fragile economies of these relatively poor nations far more than our own relatively strong one. Moreover, equity requires, even as the fact of interdependence becomes more apparent, that the *quality* of interdependence be improved, in order to eliminate "the scandal of the shocking inequality between the rich and the poor"[98] in a world divided ever more sharply between them.

253. Developing countries, moreover, often perceive themselves more as *dependent* on the industrialized countries, especially the United States, because the international system itself, as well as the way the United States acts in it, subordinates them. The prices at which they must sell their commodity exports and purchase their food and manufactured imports, the rates of interest they must pay and the terms they must meet to borrow money, the standards of economic behavior of foreign investors, the amounts and conditions of external aid, etc., are essentially determined by the industrialized world. Moreover, their traditional cultures are increasingly susceptible to the aggressive cultural penetration of Northern (especially U.S.) advertising and media programing. The developing countries are junior partners at best.

---

[98] *Instruction on Certain Aspects of the Theology of Liberation,* I:6. See also *Peace on Earth,* 130-131; and *On Human Work,* 11.

254. The basic tenets of church teaching take on a new moral urgency as we deepen our understanding of how disadvantaged large numbers of people and nations are in this interdependent world. Half the world's people, nearly two and a half billion, live in countries where the annual per capita income is $400 or less.[99] At least 800 million people in those countries live in absolute poverty, "beneath any rational definition of human decency."[100] Nearly half a billion are chronically hungry, despite abundant harvests worldwide.[101] Fifteen out of every 100 children born in those countries die before the age of five, and millions of the survivors are physically or mentally stunted. No aggregate of individual examples could portray adequately the appalling inequities within those desperately poor countries and between them and our own. And their misery is not the inevitable result of the march of history or of the intrinsic nature of particular cultures, but of human decisions and human institutions.

255. On the international economic scene three main sets of actors warrant particular attention: individual nations, which retain great influence; multilateral institutions, which channel money, power, ideas, and influence; transnational corporations and banks, which have grown dramatically in number, size, scope, and strength since World War II.[102] In less

[99] Overseas Development Council, *U.S. Policy and the Third World: Agenda 1985-1986.*

[100] Robert S. McNamara, *Address to the Board of Governors of the World Bank* (Washington, D.C.: World Bank, September 30, 1980).

[101] U.N./Food and Agricultural Organization, *Dimensions of Need,* E 9 (Rome, 1982). The U.N. World Food Council uses this figure consistently, most recently at its 11th annual meeting in Paris.

[102] Joseph Greenwald and Kenneth Flamm, *The Global Factory* (Washington, D.C.: The Brookings Institution, 1985); see also Ronald Muller and Richard Barnet, *Global Reach* (New York: Simon and Schuster, 1974); Raymond Vernon, *The Economic and Political Consequences of Multinational Enterprise* (Cambridge, Mass.: Harvard

identifiable ways trade unions, popular movements, private relief and development agencies, and regional groupings of nations also affect the global economy. The interplay among all of them sets the context for policy choices that determine whether genuine interdependence is promoted or the dependence of the disadvantaged is deepened.

256. In this arena, where fact and ethical challenges intersect, the moral task is to devise rules for the major actors that will move them toward a just international order. One of the most vexing problems is that of reconciling the transnational corporations' profit orientation with the common good that they, along with governments and their multilateral agencies, are supposed to serve.

257. The notion of interdependence erases the fading line between domestic and foreign policy. Many foreign policy decisions (for example, on trade, investment, and immigration) have direct and substantial impact on domestic constituencies in the United States. Similarly, many decisions thought of as domestic (for example, on farm policy, interest rates, the federal budget, or the deficit) have important consequences for other countries. This increasingly recognized link of domestic and foreign issues poses new empirical and moral questions for national policy.

2. The Challenge of Catholic Social Teaching

258. Catholic teaching on the international economic order recognizes this complexity, but does not provide specific solutions. Rather, we seek to ensure that moral considerations are taken into account. All of the elements of the moral perspective we have

University Press, 1972); the United Nations Center on Transnational Corporations maintains current data on these institutions.

outlined above have important implications for international relationships. (1) The demands of *Christian love* and *human solidarity* challenge all economic actors to choose community over chaos. They require a definition of political community that goes beyond national sovereignty to policies that recognize the moral bonds among all people. (2) *Basic justice* implies that all peoples are entitled to participate in the increasingly interdependent global economy in a way that ensures their freedom and dignity. When whole communities are effectively left out or excluded from equitable participation in the international order, basic justice is violated. We want a world that works fairly for all. (3) *Respect for human rights*, both political and economic, implies that international decisions, institutions, and policies must be shaped by values that are more than economic. The creation of a global order in which these rights are secure for all must be a prime objective for all relevant actors on the international stage. (4) *The special place of the poor* in this moral perspective means that meeting the basic needs of the millions of deprived and hungry people in the world must be the number one objective of international policy.

259. These perspectives constitute a call for fundamental reform in the international economic order. Whether the problem is preventing war and building peace, or addressing the needs of the poor, Catholic teaching emphasizes not only the individual conscience, but also the political, legal, and economic structures through which policy is determined and issues are adjudicated.[103] We do not seek here to evaluate the various proposals for international economic reform or deal here with economic relations between the United States and other industrialized countries. We urge, as a basic and overriding consideration, that

---

[103] *Peace on Earth*, 56–63.

both empirical and moral evidence, especially the precarious situation of the developing countries, calls for the renewal of the dialogue between the industrialized countries of the North and the developing countries of the South, with the aim of reorganizing international economic relations to establish greater equity and help meet the basic human needs of the poor majority.[104]

260. *Here, as elsewhere, the preferential option for the poor is the central priority for policy choice.* It offers a unique perspective on foreign policy in whose light U.S. relationships, especially with developing countries, can be reassessed. Standard foreign policy analysis deals with calculations of power and definitions of national interest; but the poor are, by definition, not powerful. If we are to give appropriate weight to their concerns, their needs, and their interests, we have to go beyond economic gain or national security as a starting point for the policy dialogue. We want to stand with the poor everywhere, and we believe that relations between the U.S. and developing nations should be determined in the first place by a concern for basic human needs and respect for cultural traditions.

3. The Role of the United States in the Global Economy: Constructive Choices

261. As we noted in *The Challenge of Peace*, recent popes have strongly supported the United Nations as a crucial step forward in the development and organization of the human community; we share their regret that no political entity now exists with the responsibility and power to promote the global common good, and we urge the United States to support UN

[104] *On the Development of Peoples*, 44, 58-63; quoted also by Pope John Paul II, *Origins* 14:16 (October 4, 1984): 247.

efforts to move in that direction. Building a just world economic order in the absence of such an authority demands that national governments promote public policies that increase the ability of poor nations and marginalized people to participate in the global economy. Because no other nation's economic power yet matches ours, we believe that this responsibility pertains especially to the United States; but it must be carried out in cooperation with other industrialized countries as in the case of halting the rise of the dollar. This is yet another evidence of the fact of interdependence. Joint action toward these goals not only promotes justice and reduces misery in the Third World, but also is in the interest of the United States and other industrialized nations.

262. Yet in recent years U.S. policy toward development in the Third World has become increasingly one of selective assistance based on an East-West assessment of North-South problems, at the expense of basic human needs and economic development. Such a view makes national security the central policy principle.[105] Developing countries have become largely testing grounds in the East-West struggle; they seem to have meaning or value mainly in terms of this larger geopolitical calculus. The result is that issues of human need and economic development take second place to the political-strategic argument. This tendency must be resisted.

263. Moreover, U.S. performance in North-South negotiations often casts us in the role of resisting developing-country proposals without advancing realistic ones of our own.[106] North-South dialogue is bound

---

[105] President's Commission on Security and Economic Assistance (Carlucci Commission), *A Report to the Secretary of State* (Washington, D.C., November 1983).

[106] For example: After a dozen years of negotiations, during which nearly all of the issues were resolved to U.S. satisfaction, the United States refused to sign the Law of the Seas treaty; only

to be complex, protracted, and filled with symbolic and often unrealistic demands; but the situation has now reached the point where the rest of the world expects the United States to assume a reluctant, adversarial posture in such discussions. The U.S. approach to the developing countries needs urgently to be changed; a country as large, rich, and powerful as ours has a moral obligation to lead in helping to reduce poverty in the Third World.

264. We believe that U.S. policy toward the developing world should reflect our traditional regard for human rights and our concern for social progress. In economic policy, as we noted in our pastoral letter on nuclear war, the major international economic relationships of aid, trade, finance, and investment are interdependent among themselves and illustrate the range of interdependence issues facing U.S. policy. All three of the major economic actors are active in all these relationships. Each relationship offers us the possibility of substantial, positive movement toward increasing social justice in the developing world; in each, regrettably, we fall short. It is urgent that immediate steps be taken to correct these deficiencies.

265. a. *Development Assistance:* The official development assistance that the industrialized and the oil-producing countries provide the Third World in the form of grants; low-interest, long-term loans; commodities; and technical assistance is a significant contribution to their development. Although the annual share of U.S. gross national product (GNP) devoted to foreign aid is now less than one-tenth of that of the Marshall Plan, which helped rebuild devastated but advanced European economies, we remain the largest donor country. We still play a central role in

---

the United States failed to support the U.N. infant formula resolution; the United States has not ratified the two UN Covenants on Human Rights, etc.

these resource transfers, but we no longer set an example for other donors. We lag proportionately behind most other industrial nations in providing resources and seem to care less than before about development in the Third World. Our bilateral aid has become increasingly militarized and security-related and our contributions to multilateral agencies have been reduced in recent years.[107] Not all of these changes are justifiable. The projects of the International Development Agency, for example, seem worthy of support.

266. This is a grave distortion of the priority that development assistance should command. We are dismayed that the United States, once the pioneer in foreign aid, is almost last among the seventeen industrialized nations in the Organization for Economic Cooperation and Development (OECD) in percentage of GNP devoted to aid. Reduction of the U.S. contribution to multilateral development institutions is particularly regrettable, because these institutions are often better able than the bilateral agencies to focus on the poor and reduce dependency in developing countries.[108] This is also an area in which, in the past, our leadership and example have had great influence. A more affirmative U.S. role in these institutions, which we took the lead in creating, could improve their performance, send an encouraging signal of U.S. intentions, and help reopen the dialogue on the growing poverty and dependency of the Third World.

---

[107] U.S. Agency for International Development, *Congressional Presentation, Fiscal Year 1986, Main Volume* (Washington, D.C., 1985).

[108] The clients of the International Development Association, the "soft loan window" of the World Bank, are the poorest countries. The United States insisted upon—and obtained—a 25% reduction in IDA's current (seventh) replenishment. Taking inflation into account, this meant a 40% drop in real terms at exactly the moment when developing-country debt levels are punishingly high and the prices of their export commodities are almost at rock bottom.

267. b. *Trade:* Trade continues to be a central component of international economic relations. It contributed in a major way to the rapid economic growth of many developing countries in the 1960s and 1970s and will probably continue to do so, though at a slower rate. The preferential option for the poor does not, by itself, yield a trade policy; but it does provide a frame of reference. In particular, an equitable trading system that will help the poor should allocate its benefits fairly and ensure that exports from developing countries receive fair prices reached by agreement among all trading partners. Developing nations have a right to receive a fair price for their raw materials that allows for a reasonable degree of profit.

268. Trade policy illustrates the conflicting pressures that interdependence can generate: claims of injustice from developing countries denied market access are countered by claims of injustice in the domestic economies of industrialized countries when jobs are threatened and incomes fall. Agricultural trade and a few industrial sectors present particularly acute examples of this.

269. We believe the ethical norms we have applied to domestic economic questions are equally valid here.[109] As in other economic matters, the basic questions are: Who benefits from the particular policy measure? How can any benefit or adverse impact be equitably shared? We need to examine, for example, the extent to which the success in the U.S. market of certain imports is derived from exploitative labor conditions in the exporting country, conditions that in some cases have attracted the investment in the first place. The United States should do all it can to ensure that the trading system treats the poorest segments of developing countries' societies fairly and does not lead to human rights violations. In particular the United

---

[109] See ch. II.

States should seek effective special measures under the General Agreement on Tariffs and Trade (GATT)[110] to benefit the poorest countries.

270. At the same time, U.S. workers and their families hurt by the operation of the trading system must be helped through training and other measures to adjust to changes that advance development and decrease poverty in the Third World. This is a very serious, immediate, and intensifying problem. In our judgment, adjustment assistance programs in the United States have been poorly designed and administered, and inadequately funded. A society and an economy such as ours can better adjust to trade dislocations than can poverty-ridden developing countries.

271. c. *Finance:* Aid and trade policies alone, however enlightened, do not constitute a sufficient approach to the developing countries; they must also be looked at in conjunction with international finance and investment. The debtor-creditor relationship well exemplifies both the interdependence of the international economic order and its asymmetrical character, i.e., the *dependence* of the developing countries. The aggregate external debt of the developing countries now approaches $1 trillion,[111] more than one-third of their combined GNP; this total doubled between 1979 and 1984 and continues to rise. On average, the first 20 percent of export earnings goes to service that debt without significantly reducing the principal; in some countries debt service is nearly 100

---

[110] The GATT, third of the Bretton Woods "institutions" (with the World Bank and the IMF) is in fact a treaty, monitored and supported by a secretariat located in Geneva, Switzerland. Periodic "rounds" of negotiations among its several score members, North and South, modify and extend its provisions and regulations.

[111] Debt figures have been compiled from data published by the World Bank, the IMF, and the Bank for International Settlements.

percent of such earnings, leaving scant resources available for the countries' development programs.

272. The roots of this very complex debt crisis are both historic and systemic. *Historically*, the three major economic actors share the responsibility for the present difficulty because of decisions made and actions taken during the 1970s and 1980s. In 1972 the Soviet Union purchased the entire U.S. grain surplus, and grain prices trebled. Between 1973 and 1979, the Organization of Petroleum Exporting Countries raised the price of oil eightfold and thereafter deposited most of the profits in commercial banks in the North. In order to profit from the interest-rate spread on these deposits, the banks pushed larger and larger loans on eager Third World borrowers needing funds to purchase more and more expensive oil. A second doubling of oil prices in 1979 forced many of these countries to refinance their loans and borrow more money at escalating interest rates. A global recession beginning in 1979 caused the prices of Third World export commodities to fall and thus reduced the ability to meet the increasingly burdensome debt payments out of export earnings.

273. The global *system* of finance, development, and trade established by the Bretton Woods Conference in 1944—the World Bank, the International Monetary Fund (IMF), and the GATT—was created by the North to prevent a recurrence of the economic problems that were perceived to have led to World War II. Forty years later that system seems incapable, without basic changes, of helping the debtor countries—which had no part in its creation—manage their increasingly untenable debt situation effectively and equitably. The World Bank, largest of these institutions, has been engaged primarily in lending for specific projects rather than for general economic health. The IMF was intended to be a short-term lender that would help out with temporary balance of payments, or cash-flow

problems; but in the current situation it has come to the fore as a monitor of commercial financial transactions and an evaluator of debtors' creditworthiness—and therefore the key institution for resolving these problems. The GATT, which is not an institution, had been largely supplanted, as trade monitor for the developing countries, by UNCTAD[112] in which the latter have more confidence.

274. This crisis, however, goes beyond the system; it affects people. It afflicts and oppresses large numbers of people who are already severely disadvantaged. That is the scandal: it is the poorest people who suffer most from the austerity measures required when a country seeks the IMF "seal of approval" which establishes its creditworthiness for a commercial loan (or perhaps an external aid program). It is these same people who suffer most when commodity prices fall, when food cannot be imported or they cannot buy it, and when natural disasters occur. Our commitment to the preferential option for the poor does not permit us to remain silent in these circumstances. Ways must be found to meet the immediate emergency—moratorium on payments, conversion of some dollar-denominated debt into local-currency debt, creditors' accepting a share of the burden by partially writing-down selected loans, capitalizing interest, or perhaps outright cancellation.

---

[112] The United Nations Conference on Trade and Development (UNCTAD) originated in Geneva in 1964 at a meeting convened by the U.N. to discuss trade, development, and related problems of low-income countries. It established a quadrennial meeting and created permanent machinery in the U.N. to deal with these problems. A Trade and Development Board (TDB), with standing committees, meets every two years; and there is a small secretariat to staff it. UNCTAD is viewed as representing the developing countries' continuing effort to have a larger voice in international decisions affecting trade and development and to secure more favorable terms of trade.

275. The poorest countries, especially those in sub-Saharan Africa which are least developed, most afflicted by hunger and malnutrition, and most vulnerable to commodity price declines, are in extremely perilous circumstances.[113] Although their aggregate debt of more than $100 billion (much of it owed to multilateral institutions), is about one-quarter that of Latin America, their collateral (oil, minerals, manufactures, grain, etc.) is much less adequate, their ability to service external debt much weaker, and the possibility of their rescheduling it very small. For low-income countries like these, the most useful immediate remedies are longer payment periods, lower interest rates, and modification of IMF adjustment requirements that exacerbate the already straitened circumstances of the poor.[114] Especially helpful for some African countries would be cancellation of debts owed to governments, a step already taken by some creditor nations.

276. Better off debtor countries also need to be able to adjust their debts without penalizing the poor. Although the final policy decisions about the allocation of adjustment costs belong to the debtor government, internal equity considerations should be taken into account in determining the conditions of debt rescheduling and additional lending; for example, wage reductions should not be mandated, basic public services to the poor should not be cut, and measures should be required to reduce the flight of capital. Since

---

[113] *U.S. Policy and the Third World,* Table B-5.

[114] When the IMF helps a country adjust to balance-of-payments problems (e.g., by assisting in the rescheduling of its external debt), it negotiates certain conditions with the debtor country in order to improve its immediate financial position. In general, these require the borrowing country to earn and save more. The adjustments, usually referred to as "conditionality," tend to fall most heavily on the poor through reduction of government spending on consumer subsidies and public services, and often of wages.

this debt problem, like most others, is systemic, a case-by-case approach is not sufficient: lending policies and exchange-rate considerations are not only economic questions, but are thoroughly and intensely political.

277. Beyond all this, the growing external debt that has become the overarching economic problem of the Third World also requires systemic change to provide immediate relief and to prevent recurrence. The Bretton Woods institutions do not adequately represent Third World debtors, and their policies are not dealing effectively with problems affecting those nations. These institutions need to be substantially reformed and their policies reviewed at the same time that the immediate problem of Third World debt is being dealt with. The United States should promote, support, and participate fully in such reforms and reviews. Such a role is not only morally right, but is in the economic interest of the United States; more than a third of this debt is owed to U.S. banks. The viability of the international banking system (and of those U.S. banks) depends in part on the ability of debtor countries to manage those debts. Stubborn insistence on full repayment could force them to default—which would lead to economic losses in the United States. In this connection, we should not overlook the impact of U.S. budget and trade deficits on interest rates. These high interest rates exacerbate the already difficult debt situation. They also attract capital away from investment in economic development in Third World countries.

278. d. *Foreign Private Investment:* Although direct private investment in the developing countries by U.S.-based transnational corporations has declined in recent years, it still amounts to about $60 billion and accounts for sizeable annual transfers. Such investment in developing countries should be increased, consistent with the host country's development goals and with benefits equitably distributed. Particular efforts should be made to encourage investments by

135

medium-sized and small companies, as well as to joint ventures, which may be more appropriate to the developing country's situation. For the foreseeable future, however, private investment will probably not meet the infrastructural needs of the poorest countries—roads, transportation, communications, education, health, etc.— since these do not generally show profits and therefore do not attract private capital. Yet without this infrastructure, no real economic growth can take place.

279. Direct foreign investment, risky though it may be for both the investing corporation and the developing country, can provide needed capital, technology, and managerial expertise. Care must be taken lest such investment create or perpetuate dependency, harming especially those at the bottom of the economic ladder. Investments that sustain or worsen inequities in a developing country, that help to maintain oppressive elites in power, or that increase food dependency by encouraging cash cropping for export at the expense of local needs, should be discouraged. Foreign investors, attracted by low wage rates in less developed countries, should consider both the potential loss of jobs in the home country and the potential exploitation of workers in the host country.[115] Both the products and the technologies of the investing firms should be appropriate to the developing country, neither catering just to a small number of high-income consumers, nor establishing capital-intensive processes that displace labor, especially in the agricultural sector.[116]

280. Such inequitable results, however, are not necessary consequences of transnational corporate activ-

[115] North American Coalition for Human Rights in Korea, *Testimony before the U. S. Trade Representative,* June 24, 1985.

[116] E. F. Schumacher, *Small Is Beautiful: Economics As If People Mattered* (New York: Harper and Row, 1973).

ity. Corporations can contribute to development by attracting and training high-caliber managers and other personnel, by helping organize effective marketing systems, by generating additional capital, by introducing or reinforcing financial accountability, and by sharing the knowledge gained from their own research and development activities. Although the ability of the corporations to plan, operate, and communicate across national borders without concern for domestic considerations makes it harder for governments to direct their activities toward the common good, the effort should be made; the Christian ethic is incompatible with a primary or exclusive focus on maximization of profit. We strongly urge U.S. and international support of efforts to develop a code of conduct for foreign corporations that recognizes their quasi-public character and encourages both development and the equitable distribution of their benefits. Transnational corporations should be required to adopt such a code, and to conform their behavior to its provisions.

281. e. *The World Food Problem—A Special Urgency:* These four resource transfer channels—aid, trade, finance, and investment—intersect and overlap in all economic areas, but in none more clearly than in the international food system. The largest single segment of development assistance support goes to the agricultural sector and to food aid for short-term emergencies and vulnerable groups; food constitutes one of the most critical trade sectors; developing countries have borrowed extensively in the international capital markets to finance food imports; and a substantial portion of direct private investment flows into the agricultural sector.

282. The development of U.S. agriculture has moved the United States into a dominant position in the international food system. The best way to meet the responsibilities this dominance entails is to design and

implement a U.S. food and agriculture policy that contributes to increased food security—that is, access by everyone to an adequate diet. A world with nearly half a billion hungry people is not one in which food security has been achieved. The problem of hunger has a special significance for those who read the Scriptures and profess the Christian faith. From the Lord's command to feed the hungry, to the Eucharist we celebrate as the Bread of Life, the fabric of our faith demands that we be creatively engaged in sharing the food that sustains life. There is no more basic human need. The gospel imperative takes on new urgency in a world of abundant harvests where hundreds of millions of people face starvation. Relief and prevention of their hunger cannot be left to the arithmetic of the marketplace.[117]

283. The chronic hunger of those who live literally from day to day is one symptom of the underlying problem of poverty; relieving and preventing hunger is part of a larger, coordinated strategy to attack poverty itself. People must be enabled either to grow or to buy the food they need, without depending on an indefinite dole; there is no substitute for long-term agricultural and food-system development in the nations now caught in the grip of hunger and starvation. Most authorities agree that the key to this development is the small farmers, most of whom are prevented from participating in the food system by the lack of a market incentive resulting from the poverty of the bulk of the populations and by the lack of access to productive agricultural inputs, especially land, resulting mainly from their own poverty. In these poor, food-deficit countries, no less than in our own, the small family farm deserves support and protection.

284. But recognizing the long-term problem does not dissolve the short-term obligation of the world's

---

[117] *On the Development of Peoples,* 44, 58-63.

major food-exporting nation to provide food aid sufficient to meet the nutritional needs of poor people, and to provide it not simply to dispose of surpluses but in a way that does not discourage local food production. There can be no successful solution to the problem of hunger in the world without U.S. participation in a cooperative effort that simultaneously increases food aid and launches a long-term program to help develop food self-reliance in food-deficit developing countries.

285. Hunger is often seen as being linked with the problem of population growth, as effect to cause. While this relationship is sometimes presented in oversimplified fashion, we cannot fail to recognize that the earth's resources are finite and that population tends to grow rapidly. Whether the world can provide a truly human life for twice as many people or more as now live in it (many of whose lives are sadly deficient today) is a matter of urgent concern that cannot be ignored.[118]

286. Although we do not believe that people are poor and hungry primarily because they have large families, the Church fully supports the need for all to exercise responsible parenthood. Family size is heavily dependent on levels of economic development, education, respect for women, availability of health care, and the cultural traditions of communities. Therefore, in dealing with population growth we strongly favor efforts to address these social and economic concerns.

287. Population policies must be designed as part of an overall strategy of integral human development. They must respect the freedom of parents and avoid coercion. As Pope Paul VI has said concerning population policies:

---

[118] Ibid., 37; *Pastoral Constitution*, 87.

139

It is true that too frequently an accelerated demographic increase adds its own difficulties to the problems of development: the size of the population increases more rapidly than available resources, and things are found to have reached apparently an impasse. From that moment the temptation is great to check the demographic increase by means of radical measures. It is certain that public authorities can intervene, within the limit of their competence, by favoring the availability of appropriate information and by adopting suitable measures, provided that these be in conformity with the moral law and that they respect the rightful freedom of married couples. Where the inalienable right to marriage and procreation is lacking, human dignity has ceased to exist. [119]

4. U.S. Responsibility for Reform in the International Economic System

288. The United States cannot be the sole savior of the developing world, nor are Third World countries entirely innocent with respect to their own failures or totally helpless to achieve their own destinies. Many of these countries will need to initiate positive steps to promote and sustain development and economic growth—streamline bureaucracies, account for funds, plan reasonable programs, and take further steps toward empowering their people. Progress toward development will surely require them to take some tough remedial measures as well: prevent the flight of capital, reduce borrowing, modify price discrimination against rural areas, eliminate corruption in the use of funds and other resources, and curtail spending on inefficient public enterprises. The pervasive U.S. presence in many parts of our interdependent world, however, also creates a responsibility for us to increase

---

[119] *On the Development of Peoples*, 37.

the use of U.S. economic power—not just aid—in the service of human dignity and human rights, both political and economic.

289. In particular, as we noted in our earlier letter, *The Challenge of Peace*, the contrast between expenditures on armaments and on development reflects a shift in priorities from meeting human needs to promoting "national security" and represents a massive distortion of resource allocations. In 1982, for example, the military expenditures of the industrialized countries were seventeen times larger than their foreign assistance; in 1985 the United States alone budgeted more than twenty times as much for defense as for foreign assistance, and nearly two-thirds of the latter took the form of military assistance (including subsidized arms sales) or went to countries because of their perceived strategic value to the United States.[120] *Rather than promoting U.S. arms sales, especially to countries that cannot afford them, we should be campaigning for an international agreement to reduce this lethal trade.*

290. In short, the international economic order, like many aspects of our own economy, is in crisis; the gap between rich and poor countries and between rich and poor people within countries is widening. The United States represents the most powerful single factor in the international economic equation. But even as we speak of crisis, we see an opportunity for the United States to launch a worldwide campaign for justice and economic rights to match the still incomplete, but encouraging, political democracy we have achieved in the United States with so much pain and sacrifice.

291. To restructure the international order along lines of greater equity and participation and apply the preferential option for the poor to international eco-

---

[120] Ruth Leger Sivard, *World Military and Social Expenditures 1983* (Washington D.C.: World Priorities, 1983), 23.

nomic activity will require sacrifices of at least the scope of those we have made over the years in building our own nation. We need to call again upon the qualities of leadership and vision that have marked our history when crucial choices were demanded. As Pope John Paul II said during his 1979 visit to the United States, "America, which in the past decades has demonstrated goodness and generosity in providing food for the hungry of the world, will, I am sure, be able to match this generosity with an equally convincing contribution to the establishing of a world order that will create the necessary economic and trade conditions for a more just relationship between all the nations of the world."[121]

292. We share his conviction that most of the policy issues generally called economic are, at root, moral and therefore require the application of moral principles derived from the Scriptures and from the evolving social teaching of the Church and other traditions.[122] We also recognize that we are dealing here with sensitive international issues that cross national boundaries. Nevertheless, in order to pursue justice and peace on a global scale, *we call for a U.S. international economic policy designed to empower people everywhere and enable them to continue to develop a sense of their own worth, improve the quality of their lives, and ensure that the benefits of economic growth are shared equitably.*

E. Conclusion

293. None of the issues we have addressed in this chapter can be dealt with in isolation. They are

---

[121] Pontifical Commission Justitia et Pax, *The Social Teaching of John Paul II*, 6 (October 6, 1979).

[122] *On the Development of Peoples*, 44, 58-63.

interconnected, and their resolution requires difficult trade-offs among competing interests and values. The changing international economy, for example, greatly influences efforts to achieve full employment in the United States and to maintain a healthy farm sector. Similarly, as we have noted, policies and programs to reduce unemployment and poverty must not ignore a potential inflationary impact. These complexities and trade-offs are real and must be confronted, but they are not an excuse for inaction. They should not paralyze us in our search for a more just economy.

294. Many of the reforms we have suggested in this chapter would be expensive. At a time when the United States has large annual deficits some might consider these costs too high. But this discussion must be set in the context of how our resources are allocated and the immense human and social costs of failure to act on these pressing problems. We believe that the question of providing adequate revenues to meet the needs of our nation must be faced squarely and realistically. Reforms in the tax code which close loopholes and generate new revenues, for example, are among the steps that need to be examined in order to develop a federal budget that is both fiscally sound and socially responsible. The cost of meeting our social needs must also be weighed against the $300 billion a year allocated for military purposes. Although some of these expenditures are necessary for the defense of the nation, some elements of the military budget are both wasteful and dangerous for world peace.[123] Careful reductions should be made in these areas in order to

---

[123] See "Testimony on U. S. Arms Control Policy," *Origins* 14:10 (August 9, 1984): 154ff.

free up funds for social and economic reforms. In the end, the question is not whether the United States can provide the necessary funds to meet our social needs, but whether we have the political will to do so.

Chapter IV

A NEW AMERICAN EXPERIMENT: PARTNERSHIP FOR THE PUBLIC GOOD

295. For over two hundred years the United States has been engaged in a bold experiment in democracy. The founders of the nation set out to establish justice, promote the general welfare, and secure the blessings of liberty for themselves and their posterity. Those who live in this land today are the beneficiaries of this great venture. Our review of some of the most pressing problems in economic life today shows, however, that this undertaking is not yet complete. Justice for all remains an aspiration; a fair share in the general welfare is denied to many. In addition to the particular policy recommendations made above, a long-term and more fundamental response is needed. This will call for an imaginative vision of the future that can help shape economic arrangements in creative new ways. We now want to propose some elements of such a vision and several innovations in economic structures that can contribute to making this vision a reality.

296. Completing the unfinished business of the American experiment will call for new forms of cooperation and partnership among those whose daily work is the source of the prosperity and justice of the nation. The United States prides itself on both its competitive sense of initiative and its spirit of teamwork. Today a greater spirit of partnership and team-

work is needed; competition alone will not do the job. It has too many negative consequences for family life, the economically vulnerable, and the environment. Only a renewed commitment by all to the common good can deal creatively with the realities of international interdependence and economic dislocations in the domestic economy. The virtues of good citizenship require a lively sense of participation in the commonwealth and of having obligations as well as rights within it.[1] The nation's economic health depends on strengthening these virtues among all its people, and on the development of institutional arrangements supportive of these virtues.[2]

297. The nation's founders took daring steps to create structures of participation, mutual accountability, and widely distributed power to ensure the political rights and freedoms of all. We believe that similar steps are needed today to expand economic participation, broaden the sharing of economic power, and make economic decisions more accountable to the common good. As noted above, the principle of subsidiarity states that the pursuit of economic justice must occur on all levels of society. It makes demands on communities as small as the family, as large as the

---

[1] *Octogesima Adveniens,* 24.

[2] For different analyses along these lines with quite different starting points see Martin Carnoy, Derek Shearer, and Russell Rumberger, *A New Social Contract* (New York: Harper and Row, 1983); Amatai Etzioni, *An Immodest Agenda: Reconstructing America before the Twenty-First Century* (New York: McGraw-Hill, 1983); Charles E. Lindblom, *Politics and Markets* (New York: Basic Books, 1977), esp. 346-348; George C. Lodge, *The New American Ideology* (New York: Alfred A. Knopf, 1975); Douglas Sturm, "Corporations, Constitutions, and Covenants," *Journal of the American Academy of Religion,* 41 (1973): 331-55; Lester Thurow, *The Zero-Sum Society* (New York: Basic Books, 1980), esp. ch. 1; Roberto Mangabeira Unger, *Knowledge and Politics* (New York: Free Press, 1975); George F. Will, *Statecraft as Soulcraft: What Government Does* (New York: Simon and Schuster, 1982), esp. ch. 6.

global society and on all levels in between. There are a number of ways to enhance the cooperative participation of these many groups in the task of creating this future. Since there is no single innovation that will solve all problems, we recommend careful experimentation with several possibilities that hold considerable hope for increasing partnership and strengthening mutual responsibility for economic justice.

A. Cooperation within Firms and Industries

298. A new experiment in bringing democratic ideals to economic life calls for serious exploration of ways to develop new patterns of partnership among those working in individual firms and industries.[3] Every business, from the smallest to the largest, including farms and ranches, depends on many different persons and groups for its success: workers, managers, owners or shareholders, suppliers, customers, creditors, the local community, and the wider society. Each makes a contribution to the enterprise, and each has a stake in its growth or decline. Present structures of accountability, however, do not acknowledge all these contributions or protect these stakes. A major challenge in today's economy is the development of new institutional mechanisms for accountability that also preserve the flexibility needed to respond quickly to a rapidly changing business environment.[4]

[3] *Pastoral Constitution,* 68. See *Mater et Magistra,* 75-77.
[4] Charles W. Powers provided a helpful discussion of these matters in a paper presented at a conference on the first draft of this pastoral letter sponsored by the Harvard University Divinity School and the Institute for Policy Studies, Cambridge, Massachusetts, March 29-31, 1985.

299. New forms of partnership between workers and managers are one means for developing greater participation and accountability within firms.[5] Recent experience has shown that both labor and management suffer when the adversarial relationship between them becomes extreme. As Pope Leo XIII stated, "Each needs the other completely: capital cannot do without labor, nor labor without capital."[6] The organization of firms should reflect and enhance this mutual partnership. In particular, the development of work patterns for men and women that are more supportive of family life will benefit both employees and the enterprises they work for.

300. Workers in firms and on farms are especially in need of stronger institutional protection, for their jobs and livelihood are particularly vulnerable to the decisions of others in today's highly competitive labor market. Several arrangements are gaining increasing support in the United States: profit sharing by the workers in a firm; enabling employees to become company stockholders; granting employees greater participation in determining the conditions of work; cooperative ownership of the firm by all who work within it; and programs for enabling a much larger number of Americans, regardless of their employment status, to become shareholders in successful corporations. Initiatives of this sort can enhance productivity, increase the profitability of firms, provide greater

---

[5] See John Paul II, "The Role of Business in a Changing Workplace," 3, *Origins* 15 (February 6, 1986): 567.

[6] *Rerum Novarum*, 28. For an analysis of the relevant papal teachings on institutions of collaboration and partnership, see John Cronin, *Catholic Social Principles: The Social Teaching of the Catholic Church Applied to American Economic Life* (Milwaukee: Bruce, 1950), ch. VII; Oswald von Nell-Breuning, *Reorganization of Social Economy: The Social Encyclical Developed and Explained*, trans. Bernard W. Dempsey (Milwaukee: Bruce, 1936), chs. X-XII; Jean-Yves Calvez and Jacques Perrin, *The Church and Social Justice*, trans. J. R. Kirwan (Chicago: Regnery, 1961), ch. XIX.

job security and work satisfaction for employees, and reduce adversarial relations.[7] In our 1919 Program of Social Reconstruction, we observed "the full possibilities of increased production will not be realized so long as the majority of workers remain mere wage earners. The majority must somehow become owners, at least in part, of the instruments of production."[8] We believe this judgment remains generally valid today.

301. None of these approaches provides a panacea, and all have certain drawbacks. Nevertheless we believe that continued research and experimentation with these approaches will be of benefit. Catholic social teaching has endorsed on many occasions innovative methods for increasing worker participation within firms.[9] The appropriateness of these methods will depend on the circumstances of the company or industry in question and on their effectiveness in actually increasing a genuinely cooperative approach to shaping

---

[7] Michael Conte, Arnold S. Tannenbaum, and Donna McCulloch, *Employee Ownership*, Research Report Series, Institute for Social Research (Ann Arbor, Mich.: University of Michigan, 1981); Robert A. Dahl, *A Preface to Economic Democracy* (Berkeley: University of California Press, 1985); Harvard Business School, "The Mondragon Cooperative Movement," case study prepared by David P. Ellerman (Cambridge, Mass.: Harvard Business School, n.d.); Robert Jackall and Henry M. Levin, eds., *Worker Cooperatives in America* (Berkeley: University of California Press, 1984); Derek Jones and Jan Svejnar, eds., *Participatory and Self-Managed Firms: Evaluating Economic Performance* (Lexington, Mass.: D. C. Heath, 1982); Irving H. Siegel and Edgar Weinberg, *Labor-Management Cooperation: The American Experience* (Kalamazoo, Mich.: W. E. Upjohn Institute for Employment Research, 1982); Stuart M. Speiser, "Broadened Capital Ownership—The Solution to Major Domestic and International Problems," *Journal of Post Keynesian Economics* VIII (1985): 426-434; Jaroslav Vanek, ed., *Self-Management: Economic Liberation of Man* (London: Penguin, 1975); Martin L. Weitzman, *The Share Economy* (Cambridge, Mass.: Harvard University Press, 1984).

[8] *Program of Social Reconstruction* in *Justice in the Marketplace*, 381.

[9] *Mater et Magistra*, 32, 77, 85-103; *On Human Work*, 14.

decisions. The most highly publicized examples of such efforts have been in large firms facing serious financial crises. If increased participation and collaboration can help a firm avoid collapse, why should it not give added strength to healthy businesses? Cooperative ownership is particularly worthy of consideration in new entrepreneurial enterprises.[10]

302. Partnerships between labor and management are possible only when both groups possess real freedom and power to influence decisions. This means that unions ought to continue to play an important role in moving toward greater economic participation within firms and industries. Workers rightly reject calls for less adversarial relations when they are a smokescreen for demands that labor make all the concessions. For partnership to be genuine it must be a two-way street, with creative initiative and a willingness to cooperate on all sides.

303. When companies are considering plant closures or the movement of capital, it is patently unjust to deny workers any role in shaping the outcome of these difficult choices.[11] In the heavy manufacturing sector today, technological change and international competition can be the occasion of painful decisions leading to the loss of jobs or wage reductions. While such decisions may sometimes be necessary, a collaborative and mutually accountable model of industrial organization would mean that workers not be expected to carry all the burdens of an economy in transition. Management and investors must also ac-

---

[10] For examples of worker-owned and operated enterprises supported by the Campaign for Human Development's revolving loan fund see CHD's *Annual Report* (Washington, D.C.: USCC).

[11] *Quadragesimo Anno* states the basic norm on which this conclusion is based: "It is wholly false to ascribe to property alone or to labor alone whatever has been obtained through the combined effort of both, and it is wholly unjust for either, denying the efficacy of the other, to arrogate to itself whatever has been produced" (53).

cept their share of sacrifices, especially when management is thinking of closing a plant or transferring capital to a seemingly more lucrative or competitive activity. The capital at the disposal of management is in part the product of the labor of those who have toiled in the company over the years, including currently employed workers.[12] As a minimum, workers have a right to be informed in advance when such decisions are under consideration, a right to negotiate with management about possible alternatives, and a right to fair compensation and assistance with retraining and relocation expenses should these be necessary. Since even these minimal rights are jeopardized without collective negotiation, industrial cooperation requires a strong role for labor unions in our changing economy.

304. Labor unions themselves are challenged by the present economic environment to seek new ways of doing business. The purpose of unions is not simply to defend the existing wages and prerogatives of the fraction of workers who belong to them, but also to enable workers to make positive and creative contributions to the firm, the community, and the larger society in an organized and cooperative way.[13] Such

---

[12] *On Human Work,* 12.

[13] Ibid., 20. This point was well made by John Cronin twenty-five years ago: "Even if most injustice and exploitation were removed, unions would still have a legitimate place. They are the normal voice of labor, necessary to organize social life for the common good. There is positive need for such organization today, quite independently of any social evils which may prevail. Order and harmony do not happen; they are the fruit of conscious and organized effort. While we may hope that the abuses which occasioned the rise of unions may disappear, it does not thereby follow that unions will have lost their function. On the contrary, they will be freed from unpleasant, even though temporarily necessary, tasks and able to devote all their time and efforts to a better organization of social life" *Catholic Social Principles,* 418. See also AFL-CIO Committee on the Evolution of Work, *The Future of Work* (Washington, D.C.: AFL-CIO, 1983).

contributions call for experiments with new directions in the U.S. labor movement.

305. The parts played by managers and shareholders in U.S. corporations also need careful examination. In U.S. law, the primary responsibility of managers is to exercise prudent business judgment in the interest of a profitable return to investors. But morally this legal responsibility may be exercised only within the bounds of justice to employees, customers, suppliers, and the local community. Corporate mergers and hostile takeovers may bring greater benefits to shareholders, but they often lead to decreased concern for the well-being of local communities and make towns and cities more vulnerable to decisions made from afar.

306. Most shareholders today exercise relatively little power in corporate governance.[14] Although shareholders can and should vote on the selection of corporate directors and on investment questions and other policy matters, it appears that return on investment is the governing criterion in the relation between them and management. We do not believe this is an adequate rationale for shareholder decisions. The question of how to relate the rights and responsibilities of shareholders to those of the other people and communities affected by corporate decisions is complex and insufficiently understood. We, therefore, urge serious, long-term research and experimentation in this area. More effective ways of dealing with these questions are essential to enable firms to serve the common good.

---

[14] For a classic discussion of the relative power of managers and shareholders see A. A. Berle and Gardiner C. Means, *The Modern Corporation and Private Property* (New York, Macmillan, 1932).

B. Local and Regional Cooperation

307. The context within which U.S. firms do business has direct influence on their ability to contribute to the common good. Companies and indeed whole industries are not sole masters of their own fate. Increased cooperative efforts are needed to make local, regional, national, and international conditions more supportive of the pursuit of economic justice.

308. In the principle of subsidiarity, Catholic social teaching has long stressed the importance of small- and intermediate-sized communities or institutions in exercising moral responsibility. These mediating structures link the individual to society as a whole in a way that gives people greater freedom and power to act.[15] Such groups include families, neighborhoods, church congregations, community organizations, civic and business associations, public interest and advocacy groups, community development corporations, and many other bodies. All these groups can play a crucial role in generating creative partnerships for the pursuit of the public good on the local and regional level.

309. The value of partnership is illustrated by considering how new jobs are created. The development of new businesses to serve the local community is key to revitalizing areas hit hard by unemployment.[16] The cities and regions in greatest need of these new jobs face serious obstacles in attracting enterprises that can provide them. Lack of financial resources, limited entrepreneurial skill, blighted and unsafe environments, and a deteriorating infrastructure create a vicious cycle

---

[15] Peter L. Berger and Richard John Neuhaus, *To Empower People: The Role of Mediating Structures in Public Policy* (Washington, D.C.: American Enterprise Institute, 1977).

[16] United States Small Business Administration, *1978 Annual Report* (Washington, D.C.: Government Printing Office, 1979).

that makes new investment in these areas more risky and therefore less likely.

310. Breaking out of this cycle will require a cooperative approach that draws on all the resources of the community.[17] Community development corporations can keep efforts focused on assisting those most in need. Existing business, labor, financial, and academic institutions can provide expertise in partnership with innovative entrepreneurs. New cooperative structures of local ownership will give the community or region an added stake in businesses and even more importantly give these businesses a greater stake in the community.[18] Government on the local, state, and national levels must play a significant role, especially through tax structures that encourage investment in hard hit areas and through funding aimed at conservation and basic infrastructure needs. Initiatives like these can contribute to a multilevel response to the needs of the community.

311. The Church itself can work as an effective partner on the local and regional level. First-hand knowledge of community needs and commitment to the protection of the dignity of all should put Church leaders in the forefront of efforts to encourage a community-wide cooperative strategy. Because churches

---

[17] For recent discussion from a variety of perspectives see: Robert Friedman and William Schweke, eds., *Expanding the Opportunity to Produce: Revitalizing the American Economy through New Enterprise Development: A Policy Reader* (Washington, D.C.: Corporation for New Enterprise Development, 1981); Jack A. Meyer, ed., *Meeting Human Needs: Toward a New Public Philosophy* (Washington, D.C.: American Enterprise Institute, 1982); Committee for Economic Development, *Jobs for the Hard-to-Employ: New Directions for a Public-Private Partnership* (New York: Committee for Economic Development, 1978); Gar Alperovitz and Jeff Faux, *Rebuilding America: A Blueprint for the New Economy* (New York: Pantheon Books, 1984).

[18] Christopher Mackin, *Strategies for Local Ownership and Control: A Policy Analysis* (Somerville, Mass.: Industrial Cooperative Association, 1983).

include members from many different parts of the community, they can often serve as mediator between groups who might otherwise regard each other with suspicion. We urge local church groups to work creatively and in partnership with other private and public groups in responding to local and regional problems.

C. Partnership in the Development of National Policies

312. The causes of our national economic problems and their possible solutions are the subject of vigorous debate today. The discussion often turns on the role the national government has played in creating these problems and could play in remedying them. We want to point to several considerations that could help build new forms of effective citizenship and cooperation in shaping the economic life of our country.

313. First, while economic freedom and personal initiative are deservedly esteemed in our society, we have increasingly come to recognize the inescapably social and political nature of the economy. The market is always embedded in a specific social and political context. The tax system affects consumption, saving, and investment. National monetary policy, domestic and defense programs, protection of the environment and worker safety, and regulation of international trade all shape the economy as a whole. These policies influence domestic investment, unemployment rates, foreign exchange, and the health of the entire world economy.

314. The principle of subsidiarity calls for government intervention when small or intermediate groups in society are unable or unwilling to take the steps needed to promote basic justice. Pope John XXIII observed that the growth of more complex relations of

interdependence among citizens has led to an increased role for government in modern societies.[19] This role is to work *in partnership with* the many other groups in society, helping them fulfill their tasks and responsibilities more effectively, not replacing or destroying them. The challenge of today is to move beyond abstract disputes about whether more or less government intervention is needed, to consideration of creative ways of enabling government and private groups to work together effectively.

315. It is in this light that we understand Pope John Paul II's recommendation that "society make provision for overall planning" in the economic domain.[20] Planning must occur on various levels, with the government ensuring that basic justice is protected and also protecting the rights and freedoms of all other agents. In the Pope's words:

> In the final analysis this overall concern weighs on the shoulders of the state, but it cannot mean one-sided centralization by the public authorities. Instead what is in question is a just and rational coordination within the framework of which the initiative of individuals, free groups, and local work centers and complexes must be safeguarded.[21]

316. We are well aware that the mere mention of economic planning is likely to produce a strong negative reaction in U.S. society. It conjures up images of centralized planning boards, command economies, inefficient bureaucracies, and mountains of government paperwork. It is also clear that the meaning of "planning" is open to a wide variety of interpretations and takes very different forms in various nations.[22]

---

[19] *Mater et Magistra*, 59, 62.

[20] *On Human Work*, 18.

[21] Ibid.

[22] For examples and analysis of different meanings of economic planning see Naomi Caiden and Aaron Wildavsky, *Planning and*

The Pope's words should not be construed as an endorsement of a highly centralized form of economic planning, much less a totalitarian one. His call for a "just and rational coordination" of the endeavors of the many economic actors is a call to seek creative new partnership and forms of participation in shaping national policies.

317. There are already many forms of economic planning going on within the U.S. economy today. Individuals and families plan for their economic future. Management and labor unions regularly develop both long- and short-term plans. Towns, cities, and regions frequently have planning agencies concerned with their social and economic future. When state legislatures and the U.S. Congress vote on budgets or on almost any other bill that comes before them, they are engaged in a form of public planning. Catholic social teaching does not propose a single model for political and economic life by which these levels are to be institutionally related to each other. It does insist that reasonable coordination among the different parts of the body politic is an essential condition for achieving justice. This is a moral precondition of good citizenship that applies to both individual and institutional actors. In its absence no political structure can guarantee justice in society or the economy. Effective decisions in these matters will demand greater cooperation among all citizens. To encourage our fellow citizens to consider more carefully the appropriate

---

Budgeting in Poor Countries (New York: Wiley, 1974); Robert Dahl and Charles E. Lindblom, *Politics, Economics and Welfare: Planning and Politico-Economic Systems Resolved into Basic Social Processes* (Chicago: University of Chicago Press, 1976); Stephen S. Cohen, *Modern Capitalist Planning: The French Model* (Berkeley: University of California Press, 1977); Albert Waterston, *Development Planning: Lessons of Experience* (Baltimore: Johns Hopkins Press, 1965); *Rebuilding America*, chs. 14, 15.

balance of private and local initiative with national economic policy, we make several recommendations.

318. *First, in an advanced industrial economy like ours, all parts of society, including government, must cooperate in forming national economic policies.* Taxation, monetary policy, high levels of government spending, and many other forms of governmental regulation are here to stay. A modern economy without governmental interventions of the sort we have alluded to is inconceivable. These interventions, however, should help, not replace, the contributions of other economic actors and institutions and should direct them to the common good. The development of effective new forms of partnership between private and public agencies will be difficult in a situation as immensely complex as that of the United States in which various aspects of national policy seem to contradict one another.[23] On the theoretical level, achieving greater coordination will make demands on those with the technical competence to analyze the relationship among different parts of the economy. More practically, it will require the various subgroups within our society to sharpen their concern for the common good and moderate their efforts to protect their own short-term interests.

319. *Second, the impact of national economic policies on the poor and the vulnerable is the primary criterion for judging their moral value.* Throughout this letter we have stressed the special place of the poor and the vulnerable in any ethical analysis of the U. S. economy. National economic policies that contribute to

---

[23] For example, many students of recent policy point out that monetary policy on the one hand and fiscal policies governing taxation and government expenditures on the other have been at odds with each other, with larger public deficits and high interest rates as the outcome. See Alice M. Rivlin, ed., *Economic Choices 1984* (Washington, D.C.: The Brookings Institution, 1984), esp. ch. 2.

building a true commonwealth should reflect this by standing firmly for the rights of those who fall through the cracks of our economy: the poor, the unemployed, the homeless, the displaced. Being a citizen of this land means sharing in the responsibility for shaping and implementing such policies.

320. *Third, the serious distortion of national economic priorities produced by massive national spending on defense must be remedied.* Clear-sighted consideration of the role of government shows that government and the economy are already closely intertwined through military research and defense contracts. Defense-related industries make up a major part of the U.S. economy and have intimate links with both the military and civilian government; they often depart from the competitive model of free-market capitalism. Moreover, the dedication of so much of the national budget to military purposes has been disastrous for the poor and vulnerable members of our own and other nations. The nation's spending priorities need to be revised in the interests of both justice and peace.[24]

321. We recognize that these proposals do not provide a detailed agenda. We are also aware that there is a tension between setting the goals for coherent policies and actually arriving at them by democratic means. But if we can increase the level of commitment to the common good and the virtues of citizenship in our nation, the ability to achieve these goals will greatly increase. It is these fundamental moral concerns that lead us as bishops to join the debate on national priorities.

---

[24] *The Challenge of Peace*, 270-271.

D. Cooperation at the International Level

322. If our country is to guide its international economic relationships by policies that serve human dignity and justice, we must expand our understanding of the moral responsibility of citizens to serve the common good of the entire planet. Cooperation is not limited to the local, regional, or national level. Economic policy can no longer be governed by national goals alone. The fact that the "social question has become worldwide"[25] challenges us to broaden our horizons and enhance our collaboration and sense of solidarity on the global level. The cause of democracy is closely tied to the cause of economic justice. The unfinished business of the American experiment includes the formation of new international partnerships, especially with the developing countries, based on mutual respect, cooperation, and a dedication to fundamental justice.

323. The principle of subsidiarity calls for government to intervene in the economy when basic justice requires greater social coordination and regulation of economic actors and institutions. In global economic relations, however, no international institution provides this sort of coordination and regulation. The U.N. system, including the World Bank, the International Monetary Fund, and the General Agreement on Tariffs and Trade, does not possess the requisite authority. Pope John XXIII called this institutional weakness a "structural defect" in the organization of the human community. The structures of world order, including economic ones, "no longer correspond to

---

[25] *On the Development of Peoples*, 3.

the objective requirements of the universal common good."[26]

324. Locked together in a world of limited material resources and a growing array of common problems, we help or hurt one another by the economic policies we choose. All the economic agents in our society, therefore, must consciously and deliberately attend to the good of the whole human family. We must all work to increase the effectiveness of international agencies in addressing global problems that cannot be handled through the actions of individual countries. In particular we repeat our plea made in *The Challenge of Peace* urging "that the United States adopt a stronger supportive leadership role with respect to the United Nations."[27] In the years following World War II, the United States took the lead in establishing multilateral bodies to deal with postwar economic problems. Unfortunately, in recent years this country has taken steps that have weakened rather than strengthened multilateral approaches. This is a short-sighted policy and should be reversed if the long-term interests of an interdependent globe are to be served.[28] In devising more effective arrangements for pursuing international economic justice, the overriding problem is how to get from where we are to where we ought to be. Progress toward that goal demands positive and often difficult action by corporations, banks, labor unions, governments, and other major actors on the international stage. But whatever the difficulty, the need to give priority to alleviating poverty in developing countries is undeniable; and the cost of continued inaction can be counted in human lives lost or stunted, talents wasted, opportunities foregone, misery and suffering prolonged, and injustice condoned.

---

[26] *Peace on Earth*, 134-135.
[27] *The Challenge of Peace*, 268.
[28] See Robert O. Keohane and Joseph S. Nye, Jr., "Two Cheers for Multilateralism," *Foreign Policy* 60 (Fall 1985): 148-167.

325. Self-restraint and self-criticism by all parties are necessary first steps toward strengthening the international structures to protect the common good. Otherwise, growing interdependence will lead to conflict and increased economic threats to human dignity. This is an important long-term challenge to the economic future of this country and its place in the emerging world economic community.

Chapter V

A COMMITMENT
TO THE FUTURE

326. Because Jesus' command to love our neighbor is universal, we hold that the life of each person on this globe is sacred. This commits us to bringing about a just economic order where all, without exception, will be treated with dignity and to working in collaboration with those who share this vision. The world is complex and this may often tempt us to seek simple and self-centered solutions; but as a community of disciples we are called to a new hope and to a new vision that we must live without fear and without oversimplification. Not only must we learn more about our moral responsibility for the larger economic issues that touch the daily life of each and every person on this planet, but we also want to help shape the Church as a model of social and economic justice. Thus, this chapter deals with the Christian vocation in the world today, the special challenges to the Church at this moment of history, ways in which the themes of this letter should be followed up, and a call to the kind of commitment that will be needed to reshape the future.

A. The Christian Vocation in the World Today

327. This letter has addressed many matters commonly regarded as secular, for example, employment rates, income levels, and international economic relationships. Yet, the affairs of the world, including economic ones, cannot be separated from the spiritual hunger of the human heart. We have presented the biblical vision of humanity and the Church's moral and religious tradition as a framework for asking the deeper questions about the meaning of economic life and for actively responding to them. But words alone are not enough. The Christian perspective on the meaning of economic life must transform the lives of individuals, families, in fact, our whole culture. The Gospel confers on each Christian the vocation to love God and neighbor in ways that bear fruit in the life of society. That vocation consists above all in a change of heart: a conversion expressed in praise of God and in concrete deeds of justice and service.

1. Conversion

328. The transformation of social structures begins with and is always accompanied by a conversion of the heart.[1] As disciples of Christ each of us is called to a deep personal conversion and to "action on behalf of justice and participation in the transformation of the world."[2] By faith and baptism we are fashioned into a "new creature"; we are filled with the Holy Spirit and a new love that compels us to seek out a new profound relationship with God, with the human

---

[1] *Reconciliation and Penance*, 13.

[2] *Justice in the World*, 6.

family, and with all created things.[3] Renouncing self-centered desires, bearing one's daily cross, and imitating Christ's compassion, all involve a personal struggle to control greed and selfishness, a personal commitment to reverence one's own human dignity and the dignity of others by avoiding self-indulgence and those attachments that make us insensitive to the conditions of others and that erode social solidarity. Christ warned us against attachments to material things, against total self-reliance, against the idolatry of accumulating material goods and seeking safety in them. We must take these teachings seriously and in their light examine how each of us lives and acts towards others. But personal conversion is not gained once and for all. It is a process that goes on through our entire life. Conversion, moreover, takes place in the context of a larger faith community: through baptism into the Church, through common prayer, and through our activity with others on behalf of justice.

2. Worship and Prayer

329. Challenging U.S. economic life with the Christian vision calls for a deeper awareness of the integral connection between worship and the world of work. Worship and common prayer are the wellsprings that give life to any reflection on economic problems and that continually call the participants to greater fidelity to discipleship. To worship and pray to the God of the universe is to acknowledge that the healing love of God extends to all persons and to every part of existence, including work, leisure, money, economic and political power and their use, and to all those practical policies that either lead to justice or impede it. Therefore, when Christians come together in prayer,

---

[3] Medellín Documents: *Justice* (1968), 4.

they make a commitment to carry God's love into all these areas of life.

330. The unity of work and worship finds expression in a unique way in the Eucharist. As people of a new covenant, the faithful hear God's challenging word proclaimed to them—a message of hope to the poor and oppressed—and they call upon the Holy Spirit to unite all into one body of Christ. For the Eucharist to be a living promise of the fullness of God's Kingdom, the faithful must commit themselves to living as redeemed people with the same care and love for all people that Jesus showed. The body of Christ which worshipers receive in Communion is also a reminder of the reconciling power of his death on the Cross. It empowers them to work to heal the brokenness of society and human relationships and to grow in a spirit of self-giving for others.

331. The liturgy teaches us to have grateful hearts: to thank God for the gift of life, the gift of this earth, and the gift of all people. It turns our hearts from self-seeking to a spirituality that sees the signs of true discipleship in our sharing of goods and working for justice. By uniting us in prayer with all the people of God, with the rich and the poor, with those near and dear, and with those in distant lands, liturgy challenges our way of living and refines our values. Together in the community of worship, we are encouraged to use the goods of this earth for the benefit of all. In worship and in deeds for justice, the Church becomes a "sacrament," a visible sign of that unity in justice and peace that God wills for the whole of humanity.[4]

---

[4] *Dogmatic Constitution on the Church*, 1; *Pastoral Constitution*, 42, 45; *Constitution on the Liturgy*, 26; *Decree on the Church's Missionary Activity*, 5; *Liturgy and Social Justice*, ed. by Mark Searle, (Collegeville, Minn.: Liturgical Press, 1980); National Conference of Catholic Bishops, *The Church at Prayer* (Washington, D.C.: USCC Office of Publishing and Promotion Services, 1983).

3. Call to Holiness in the World

332. Holiness is not limited to the sanctuary or to moments of private prayer; it is a call to direct our whole heart and life toward God and according to God's plan for this world. For the laity holiness is achieved in the midst of the world, in family, in community, in friendships, in work, in leisure, in citizenship. Through their competency and by their activity, lay men and women have the vocation to bring the light of the Gospel to economic affairs, "so that the world may be filled with the Spirit of Christ and may more effectively attain its destiny in justice, in love, and in peace."[5]

333. But as disciples of Christ we must constantly ask ourselves how deeply the biblical and ethical vision of justice and love permeates our thinking. How thoroughly does it influence our way of life? We may hide behind the complexity of the issues or dismiss the significance of our personal contribution; in fact, each one has a role to play, because every day each one makes economic decisions. Some, by reason of their work or their position in society, have a vocation to be involved in a more decisive way in those decisions that affect the economic well-being of others. They must be encouraged and sustained by all in their search for greater justice.

334. At times we will be called upon to say no to the cultural manifestations that emphasize values and aims that are selfish, wasteful, and opposed to the Scriptures. Together we must reflect on our personal and family decisions and curb unnecessary wants in order to meet the needs of others. There are many questions we must keep asking ourselves: Are we becoming ever more wasteful in a "throw-away" so-

---

[5] *Dogmatic Constitution on the Church,* 36.

ciety? Are we able to distinguish between our true needs and those thrust on us by advertising and a society that values consumption more than saving? All of us could well ask ourselves whether as a Christian prophetic witness we are not called to adopt a simpler lifestyle, in the face of the excessive accumulation of material goods that characterizes an affluent society.

335. Husbands and wives, in particular, should weigh their needs carefully and establish a proper priority of values as they discuss the questions of both parents working outside the home and the responsibilities of raising children with proper care and attention. At times we will be called as individuals, as families, as parishes, as Church, to identify more closely with the poor in their struggle for participation and to close the gap of understanding between them and the affluent. By sharing the perspectives of those who are suffering, we can come to understand economic and social problems in a deeper way, thus leading us to seek more durable solutions.

336. In the workplace the laity are often called to make tough decisions with little information about the consequences that such decisions have on the economic lives of others. Such times call for collaborative dialogue together with prayerful reflection on Scripture and ethical norms. The same can be said of the need to elaborate policies that will reflect sound ethical principles and that can become a part of our political and social system. Since this is a part of the lay vocation and its call to holiness, the laity must seek to instill a moral and ethical dimension into the public debate on these issues and help enunciate the ethical questions that must be faced. To weigh political options according to criteria that go beyond efficiency and expediency requires prayer, reflection, and dialogue on all the ethical norms involved. Holiness for the laity will involve all the sacrifices needed to lead

such a life of prayer and reflection within a worshiping and supporting faith community. In this way the laity will bridge the gap that so easily arises between the moral principles that guide the personal life of the Christian and the considerations that govern decisions in society in the political forum and in the marketplace.

4. Leisure

337. Some of the difficulty in bringing Christian faith to economic life in the United States today results from the obstacles to establishing a balance of labor and leisure in daily life. Tedious and boring work leads some to look for fulfillment only during time off the job. Others have become "workaholics," people who work compulsively and without reflection on the deeper meaning of life and their actions. The quality and pace of work should be more human in scale enabling people to experience the dignity and value of their work and giving them time for other duties and obligations. This balance is vitally important for sustaining the social, political, educational, and cultural structures of society. The family, in particular, requires such balance. Without leisure there is too little time for nurturing marriages, for developing parent-child relationships, and for fulfilling commitments to other important groups: the extended family, the community of friends, the parish, the neighborhood, schools, and political organizations. Why is it one hears so little today about shortening the work week, especially if both parents are working? Such a change would give them more time for each other, for their children, and for their other social and political responsibilities.

338. Leisure is connected to the whole of one's value system and influenced by the general culture one lives in. It can be trivialized into boredom and

laziness, or end in nothing but a desire for greater consumption and waste. For disciples of Christ, the use of leisure may demand being countercultural. The Christian tradition sees in leisure, time to build family and societal relationships and an opportunity for communal prayer and worship, for relaxed contemplation and enjoyment of God's creation, and for the cultivation of the arts which help fill the human longing for wholeness. Most of all, we must be convinced that economic decisions affect our use of leisure and that such decisions are also to be based on moral and ethical considerations. In this area of leisure we must be on our guard against being swept along by a lack of cultural values and by the changing fads of an affluent society. In the creation narrative God worked six days to create the world and rested on the seventh (Gn 2:1-4). We must take that image seriously and learn how to harmonize action and rest, work and leisure, so that both contribute to building up the person as well as the family and community.

B. Challenges to the Church

339. The Church is all the people of God, gathered in smaller faith communities, guided and served by a pope and a hierarchy of bishops, ministered to by priests, deacons, religious, and laity, through visible institutions and agencies. Church is, thus, primarily a communion of people bonded by the Spirit with Christ as their Head, sustaining one another in love, and acting as a sign or sacrament in the world. By its nature it is people called to a transcendent end; but, it is also a visible social institution functioning in this world. According to their calling, members participate in the mission and work of the Church and share, to

varying degrees, the responsibility for its institutions and agencies.[6]

At this moment in history, it is particularly important to emphasize the responsibilities of the whole Church for education and family life.

1. Education

340. We have already emphasized the commitment to quality education that is necessary if the poor are to take their rightful place in the economic structures of our society. We have called the Church to remember its own obligation in this regard and we have endorsed support for improvements in public education.

341. The educational mission of the Church is not only to the poor but to all its members. We reiterate our 1972 statement: "Through education, the Church seeks to prepare its members to proclaim the Good News and to translate this proclamation into action. Since the Christian vocation is a call to transform oneself and society with God's help, the educational efforts of the Church must encompass the twin purposes of personal sanctification and social reform in the light of Christian values."[7] Through her educational mission the Church seeks: to integrate knowledge about this world with revelation about God; to understand God's relationship to the human race and its ultimate destiny in the Kingdom of God; to build up human communities of justice and peace; and to teach the value of all creation. By inculcating these values the educational system of the Church contributes to society and to social justice. Economic questions are, thus, seen as a part of a larger vision of the human

---

[6] *Justice in the World*, 41.

[7] National Conference of Catholic Bishops, *To Teach as Jesus Did*, A Pastoral Message on Education (Washington, D.C.: USCC Office of Publishing and Promotion Services, 1972), 7.

person and the human family, the value of this created earth, and the duties and responsibilities that all have toward each other and toward this universe.

342. For these reasons the Church must incorporate into all levels of her educational system the teaching of social justice and the biblical and ethical principles that support it. We call on our universities, in particular, to make Catholic social teaching, and the social encyclicals of the popes a part of their curriculum, especially for those whose vocation will call them to an active role in U.S. economic and political decision making. Faith and technological progress are not opposed one to another, but this progress must not be channeled and directed by greed, self-indulgence, or novelty for its own sake, but by values that respect human dignity and foster social solidarity.

343. The Church has always held that the first task and responsibility for education lies in the hands of parents: they have the right to choose freely the schools or other means necessary to educate their children in the faith.[8] The Church also has consistently held that public authorities must ensure that public subsidies for the education of children are allocated so that parents can freely choose to exercise this right without incurring unjust burdens. This parental right should not be taken from them. We call again for equitable sharing in public benefits for those parents who choose private and religious schools for their children. Such help should be available especially for low-income parents. Though many of these parents sacrifice a great deal for their children's education, others are effectively deprived of the possibility of exercising this right.

---

[8] Cf. Vatican Council II, *Declaration on Christian Education*, 3, 6. See also, *Charter of the Rights of the Family*, 5b; *Instruction on Christian Freedom and Liberation*, 94.

2. Supporting the Family

344. Economic life has a profound effect on all social structures and particularly on the family. A breakdown of family life often brings with it hardship and poverty. Divorce, failure to provide support to mothers and children, abandonment of children, pregnancies out of wedlock, all contribute to the amount of poverty among us. Though these breakdowns of marriage and the family are more visible among the poor, they do not affect only that one segment of our society. In fact, one could argue that many of these breakdowns come from the false values found among the more affluent—values which ultimately pervade the whole of society.

345. More studies are needed to probe the possible connections between affluence and family and marital breakdowns. The constant seeking for self-gratification and the exaggerated individualism of our age, spurred on by false values often seen in advertising and on television, contribute to the lack of firm commitment in marriage and to destructive notions of responsibility and personal growth.[9]

346. With good reason, the Church has traditionally held that the family is the basic building block of any society. In fighting against economic arrangements that weaken the family, the Church contributes to the well-being of society. The same must be said of the Church's teaching on responsible human sexuality and its relationship to marriage and family. Economic

---

[9] Pope John Paul II, *On the Family* (Washington, D.C.: USCC Office of Publishing and Promotion Services, 1981), 6. See also Robert N. Bellah, Richard Madsen, William M. Sullivan, Ann Swidler, Steven M. Tipton, *Habits of the Heart: Individualism and Commitment in American Life* (Berkeley: University of California Press, 1985); *The Family Today and Tomorrow: The Church Addresses Her Future* (Boston, Mass.: The Pope John Center, 1985).

arrangements must support the family and promote its solidity.

3. The Church as Economic Actor

347. Although all members of the Church are economic actors every day in their individual lives, they also play an economic role united together as Church. On the parish and diocesan level, through its agencies and institutions, the Church employs many people; it has investments; it has extensive properties for worship and mission. *All the moral principles that govern the just operation of any economic endeavor apply to the Church and its agencies and institutions; indeed the Church should be exemplary.* The Synod of Bishops in 1971 worded this challenge most aptly: "While the Church is bound to give witness to justice, she recognizes that anyone who ventures to speak to people about justice must first be just in their eyes. Hence, we must undertake an examination of the modes of acting and of the possessions and lifestyle found within the Church herself."[10]

348. Catholics in the United States can be justly proud of their accomplishments in building and maintaining churches and chapels, and an extensive system of schools, hospitals, and charitable institutions. Through sacrifices and personal labor our immigrant ancestors built these institutions. For many decades religious orders of women and men taught in our schools and worked in our hospitals with very little remuneration. Right now, we see the same spirit of generosity among the religious and lay people even as we seek to pay more adequate salaries.

349. We would be insincere were we to deny a need for renewal in the economic life of the Church itself

---

[10] *Justice in the World*, 40.

174

and for renewed zeal on the part of the Church in examining its role in the larger context of reinforcing in U.S. society and culture those values that support economic justice.[11]

350. We select here five areas for special reflection: (1) wages and salaries, (2) rights of employees, (3) investments and property, (4) works of charity, and (5) working for economic justice.

351. We bishops commit ourselves to the principle that those who serve the Church—laity, clergy, and religious—should receive a sufficient livelihood and the social benefits provided by responsible employers in our nation. These obligations, however, cannot be met without the increased contributions of all the members of the Church. We call on all to recognize their responsibility to contribute monetarily to the support of those who carry out the public mission of the Church. Sacrificial giving or tithing by all the People of God would provide the funds necessary to pay these adequate salaries for religious and lay people; the lack of funds is the usual underlying cause for the lack of adequate salaries. The obligation to sustain the Church's institutions—education and health care, social service agencies, religious education programs, care of the elderly, youth ministry, and the like—falls on all the members of the community because of their baptism; the obligation is not just on the users or on those who staff them. Increased resources are also needed for the support of elderly members of religious communities. These dedicated women and men have not always asked for or received the stipends and pensions that would have assured their future. It would be a breach of our obligations to them to let them or their communities face retirement without adequate funds.

---

[11] *Dogmatic Constitution on the Church*, 8.

352. Many volunteers provide services to the Church and its mission which cannot be measured in dollars and cents. These services are important to the life and vitality of the Church in the United States and carry on a practice that has marked the history of the Church in this country since its founding. In this tradition, we ask young people to make themselves available for a year or more of voluntary service before beginning their training for more specific vocations in life; we also recommend expanding voluntary service roles for retired persons; we encourage those who have accepted this challenge.

353. All church institutions must also fully recognize the rights of employees to organize and bargain collectively with the institution through whatever association or organization they freely choose.[12] In the light of new creative models of collaboration between labor and management described earlier in this letter, we challenge our church institutions to adopt new fruitful modes of cooperation. Although the Church has its own nature and mission that must be respected and fostered, we are pleased that many who are not of our faith, but who share similar hopes and aspirations for the human family, work for us and with us in achieving this vision. In seeking greater justice in wages, we recognize the need to be alert particularly to the continuing discrimination against women throughout Church and society, especially reflected in both the inequities of salaries between women and men and in the concentration of women in jobs at the lower end of the wage scale.

354. Individual Christians who are shareholders and those responsible within church institutions that own stocks in U.S. corporations must see to it that

---

[12] National Conference of Catholic Bishops, *Health and Health Care* (Washington, D.C.: USCC Office of Publishing and Promotion Services, 1981), 50.

the invested funds are used responsibly. Although it is a moral and legal fiduciary responsibility of the trustees to ensure an adequate return on investment for the support of the work of the Church, their stewardship embraces broader moral concerns. As part-owners, they must cooperate in shaping the policies of those companies through dialogue with management, through votes at corporate meetings, through the introduction of resolutions, and through participation in investment decisions. We praise the efforts of dioceses and other religious and ecumenical bodies that work together toward these goals. We also praise efforts to develop alternative investment policies, especially those which support enterprises that promote economic development in depressed communities and which help the Church respond to local and regional needs.[13] When the decision to divest seems unavoidable, it should be done after prudent examination and with a clear explanation of the motives.

355. The use of church property demands special attention today. Changing demographic patterns have left many parishes and institutions with empty or partially used buildings. The decline in the number of religious who are teaching in the schools and the reduction in the number of clergy often result in large residences with few occupants. In this regard, the Church must be sensitive to the image the possession of such large facilities often projects, namely, that it is wealthy and extravagant in the use of its resources. This image can be overcome only by clear public accountability of its financial holdings, of its properties and their use, and of the services it renders to its members and to society at large. We support and encourage the creative use of these facilities by many parishes and dioceses to serve the needs of the poor.

---

[13] See ch. IV of this pastoral letter.

356. The Church has a special call to be a servant of the poor, the sick, and the marginalized, thereby becoming a true sign of the Church's mission—a mission shared by every member of the Christian community. The Church now serves many such people through one of the largest private human services delivery systems in the country. The networks of agencies, institutions, and programs provide services to millions of persons of all faiths. Still we must be reminded that in our day our Christian concerns must increase and extend beyond our borders, because everyone in need is our neighbor. We must also be reminded that charity requires more than alleviating misery. It demands genuine love for the person in need. It should probe the meaning of suffering and provoke a response that seeks to remedy causes. True charity leads to advocacy.

357. Yet charity alone is not a corrective to all economic social ills. All citizens, working through various organizations of society and through government, bear the responsibility of caring for those who are in need. The Church, too, through all its members individually and through its agencies, must work to alleviate injustices that prevent some from participating fully in economic life. Our experience with the Campaign for Human Development confirms our judgment about the validity of self-help and empowerment of the poor. The campaign, which has received the positive support of American Catholics since it was launched in 1970, provides a model that we think sets a high standard for similar efforts. We bishops know of the many faithful in all walks of life who use their skills and their compassion to seek innovative ways to carry out the goals we are proposing in this letter. As they do this, they *are* the Church acting for economic justice. At the same time, we hope they will join together with us and their priests to influence our society so that even more steps can be taken to alleviate injus-

tices. Grassroots efforts by the poor themselves, helped by community support, are indispensable. The entire Christian community can learn much from the way our deprived brothers and sisters assist each other in their struggles.

358. In addition to being an economic actor, the Church is a significant cultural actor concerned about the deeper cultural roots of our economic problems. As we have proposed a new experiment in collaboration and participation in decision making by all those affected at all levels of U. S. society, so we also commit the Church to become a model of collaboration and participation.

C. The Road Ahead

359. The completion of a letter such as this one is but the beginning of a long process of education, discussion and action; its contents must be brought to all members of the Church and of society.

360. In this respect we mentioned the twofold aim of this pastoral letter: to help Catholics form their consciences on the moral dimensions of economic decision making and to articulate a moral perspective in the general societal and political debate that surrounds these questions. These two purposes help us to reflect on the different ways the institutions and ministers of the Church can assist the laity in their vocation in the world. Renewed emphasis on Catholic social teaching in our schools, colleges, and universities; special seminars with corporate officials, union leaders, legislators, bankers, and the like; the organization of small groups composed of people from different ways of life to meditate together on the Gospel and ethical norms; speakers' bureaus; family programs; clearinghouses of available material; pulpit aids for

priests; diocesan television and radio programs; research projects in our universities—all of these are appropriate means for continued discussion and action. Some of these are done best on the parish level, others by the state Catholic conferences, and others by the National Conference of Catholic Bishops. These same bodies can assist the laity in the many difficult decisions that deal with political options that affect economic decisions. Where many options are available, it must be the concern of all in such debates that we as Catholics do not become polarized. All must be challenged to show how the decisions they make and the policies they suggest flow from the ethical moral vision outlined here. As new problems arise, we hope through our continual reflection that we will be able to help refine Catholic social teaching and contribute to its further development.

361. We call upon our priests, in particular, to continue their study of these issues, so that they can proclaim the gospel message in a way that not only challenges the faithful but also sustains and encourages their vocation in and to the world. Priestly formation in our seminaries will also have to prepare candidates for this role.

362. We wish to emphasize the need to undertake research into many of the areas this document could not deal with in depth and to continue exploration of those we have dealt with. We encourage our Catholic universities, foundations, and other institutions to assist in these necessary projects. The following areas for further research are merely suggestive, not exhaustive: the impact of arms production and large military spending on the domestic economy and on culture; arms production and sales as they relate to Third World poverty; tax reforms to express the preferential option for the poor; the rights of women and minorities in the work force; the development of communications technology and its global influences; ro-

botics, automation, and reduction of defense industries as they will affect employment; the economy and the stability of the family; legitimate profit versus greed; securing economic rights; environmental and ecological questions; future roles of labor and unions; international financial institutions and Third World debt; our national deficit; world food problems; "full employment" and its implementation; plant closings and dealing with the human costs of an evolving economy; cooperatives and new modes of sharing; welfare reform and national eligibility standards; income support systems; concentration of land ownership; assistance to Third World nations; migration and its effects; population policies and development; the effects of increased inequality of incomes in society.

D. Commitment to a Kingdom of Love and Justice

363. Confronted by this economic complexity and seeking clarity for the future, we can rightly ask ourselves one single question: How does our economic system affect the lives of people—*all* people? Part of the American dream has been to make this world a better place for people to live in; at this moment of history that dream must include everyone on this globe. Since we profess to be members of a "catholic" or universal Church, we all must raise our sights to a concern for the well-being of everyone in the world. Third World debt becomes our problem. Famine and starvation in sub-Saharan Africa become our concern. Rising military expenditures everywhere in the world become part of our fears for the future of this planet. We cannot be content if we see ecological neglect or the squandering of natural resources. In this letter we bishops have spoken often of economic interdepen-

dence; now is the moment when all of us must confront the reality of such economic bonding and its consequences and see it as a moment of grace—a *kairos*—that can unite all of us in a common community of the human family. We commit ourselves to this global vision.

364. We cannot be frightened by the magnitude and complexity of these problems. We must not be discouraged. In the midst of this struggle, it is inevitable that we become aware of greed, laziness, and envy. No utopia is possible on this earth; but as believers in the redemptive love of God and as those who have experienced God's forgiving mercy, we know that God's providence is not and will not be lacking to us today.

365. The fulfillment of human needs, we know, is not the final purpose of the creation of the human person. We have been created to share in the divine life through a destiny that goes far beyond our human capabilities and before which we must in all humility stand in awe. Like Mary in proclaiming her *Magnificat*, we marvel at the wonders God has done for us, how God has raised up the poor and the lowly and promised great things for them in the Kingdom. God now asks of us sacrifices and reflection on our reverence for human dignity—in ourselves and in others—and on our service and discipleship, so that the divine goal for the human family and this earth can be fulfilled. Communion with God, sharing God's life, involves a mutual bonding with all on this globe. Jesus taught us to love God and one another and that the concept of neighbor is without limit. We know that we are called to be members of a new covenant of love. We have to move from our devotion to independence, through an understanding of interdependence, to a commitment to human solidarity. That challenge must find its realization in the kind of com-

munity we build among us. Love implies concern for all—especially the poor—and a continued search for those social and economic structures that permit everyone to share in a community that is a part of a redeemed creation (Rom 8:21-23).

SELECTED BIBLIOGRAPHY

Papal and Vatican Documents

Pope Leo XIII. *Rerum Novarum (On the Condition of Workers)*, May 15, 1891.

Pope Pius XI. *Quadragesimo Anno (On Reconstructing the Social Order)*, May 15, 1931.

————. *Divini Redemptoris (On Atheistic Communism)*, March 19, 1937.

Pope John XXIII. *Mater et Magistra (On Christianity and Social Progress)*, May 15, 1961.

————. *Pacem in Terris (On Establishing Universal Peace in Truth, Justice, Charity and Liberty*, April 11, 1963.

Second Vatican Council. *Lumen Gentium (Dogmatic Constitution on the Church)*, November 21, 1964.

————. *Dei Verbum (Dogmatic Constitution on Divine Revelation)*, November 18, 1965.

————. *Dignitatis Humanae (Declaration on Religious Freedom)*, December 7, 1965.

————. *Gaudium et Spes (Pastoral Constitution on the Church in the Modern World)*, December 7, 1965.

Pope Paul VI, *Populorum Progressio (On Promoting the Development of Peoples)*, March 26, 1967.

————. *Octogesima Adveniens (On the Occasion of the Eightieth Anniversary of the Encyclical Rerum Novarum)*, May 14, 1971.

————. *Evangelii Nuntiandi (On Evangelization in the Modern World)*, December 8, 1975.

Synod of Bishops, *Justice in the World (Justitia in Mundo)*, 1971.

Pope John Paul II, *Redemptor Hominis (Redeemer of Man)*, March 4, 1979.

_____. *Dives in Misericordia (Rich in Mercy)*, November 30, 1980.

_____. *Laborem Exercens (On Human Work)*, September 14, 1981.

_____. *Salvifici Doloris (On the Christian Meaning of Human Suffering)*, February 11, 1984.

Collections and Commentaries

Abbott, Walter M., SJ, ed. *The Documents of Vatican II*, Very Rev. Msgr. Joseph Gallagher, trans. New York: America Press, 1966.

Baum, Gregory. *The Priority of Labor: A Commentary on "Laborem Exercens."* New York: Paulist Press, 1982.

Benestad, J. Brian, Ph.D., and Francis J. Butler, S.T.D., eds., *Quest for Justice: A Compendium of the Statements of the United States Catholic Bishops on the Political and Social Order, 1966-1980.* Washington, D.C.: USCC Office of Publishing and Promotion Services, 1981.

Byers, David M., ed. *Justice in the Marketplace: Collected Statements of the Vatican and the U.S. Catholic Bishops on Economic Policy, 1891-1984*, with commentary by John T. Pawlikowski, OSM, Ph.D. Washington, D.C.: USCC Office of Publishing and Promotion Services, 1985.

Calvez, Jean-Yves. *The Social Thought of John XXIII: "Mater et Magistra,"* George McKenzie, trans. Chicago: Regnery, 1964.

Calvez, Jean-Yves and Jacques Perrin. *The Church and Social Justice*, J. R. Kirwan, trans. Chicago: Regnery, 1961.

Camp, Richard L. *The Papal Ideology of Social Reform*. Leiden: Brill, 1969.

Cronin, John F. *Catholic Social Principles*. Milwaukee: Bruce, 1950.

Dorr, Donald. *Option for the Poor: A Hundred Years of Vatican Social Teaching*. Dublin: Gillord McMillan/ Maryknoll, N.Y.: Orbis Books, 1983.

Flannery, Austin, OP, ed. *Vatican Council II: The Conciliar and Post Conciliar Documents*. Vatican Collection, Vol. 1. Northport, N.Y.: Costello Publishing Company, 1975.

_____. *Vatican Council II: More Post Conciliar Documents*. Vatican Collection, Vol. 2. Northport, N.Y.: Costello Publishing Company, 1982.

Gibbons, William J., ed. *Seven Great Encyclicals*. New York: Paulist Press, 1963.

Gremillion, Joseph, ed. *The Gospel of Peace and Justice: Catholic Social Teaching Since Pope John XXIII*. Maryknoll, N.Y.: Orbis Books, 1976.

Gudorf, Christine, E. *Catholic Social Teaching on Liberation Themes*. Lanham, Md.: University Press of America, 1980.

Heckel, Roger. *The Social Teaching of John Paul II: The Use of the Expression "Social Doctrine" of the Church*. Vatican City: Pontifical Commission Justitia et Pax, 1980.

Holland, Joe and Peter Henriot. *Social Analysis: Linking Faith and Justice*. Washington, D.C.: Center for Concern, 1980.

Hollenbach, David. *Claims in Conflict*. New York: Paulist Press, 1979.

Moody, Joseph N. *Church and Society: Catholic Social and Political Thought and Movements, 1789-1950*. New York: Arts, 1953.

Nell-Breuning, Oswald von. *Reorganization of Social Economy*, B. W. Dempsey, trans. Milwaukee: Bruce, 1936.

Novak, Michael. *Freedom with Justice: Catholic Social Thought and Liberal Institutions*. San Francisco: Harper and Row, 1984.

O'Brien, David J. and Thomas A. Shannon, eds. *Renewing the Earth: Catholic Documents on Peace, Justice, and Liberation*. Garden City, N.Y.: Doubleday, 1977.

Ryan, John A. *A Living Wage*. New York: Macmillan, 1906.

_____. *Distributive Justice*, Third Edition. New York: Macmillan, 1942.

Schotte, Jan P. *Reflections on "Laborem Exercens."* (Vatican City: Pontifical Commission Justitia et Pax, 1982.

Vidler, Alec R. *A Century of Social Catholicism*. London: SPCK, 1964.

Walsh, Michael and Brian Davies, eds. *Proclaiming Justice and Peace: Documents from John XXIII-John Paul II*. Mystic, Conn.: Twenty-Third Publications, 1984.